# Doggy Knits

Anna Tillman

# Doggy Knits

Over 20 coat designs for handsome hounds and perfect pooches

T.F.H. Publications
President/CEO: Glen S. Axelrod
Executive Vice President: Mark E. Johnson
Publisher: Christopher T. Reggio
Production Manager: Kathy Bontz
US Editor: Amanda Pisani

T.F.H. Publications, Inc.
One TFH Plaza
Third and Union Avenues
Neptune City, NJ 07753

Anna Tillman asserts the moral right to be identified as the author
of this work.

Printed and bound in China
06 07 08 09 10 1 3 5 7 9 8 6 4 2

Library of Congress Cataloging-in-Publication Data
Tillman, Anna.
  Doggy knits: over 20 coat designs for handsome hounds and
perfect pooches / Anna Tillman.
        p. cm.
  Includes index.
  ISBN 0-7938-0600-3 (alk. paper)
  1. Knitting--Patterns. 2.  Dogs--Equipment and supplies. 3.
Sweaters.  I. Title.
  TT825.T534 2006
  746.43'2041--dc22
  2006011661

This book has been published with the intent to provide accurate
and authoritative information in regard to the subject matter within.
While every precaution has been taken in preparation of this book,
the author and publisher expressly disclaim responsibility for any
errors, omissions, or adverse effects arising from the use or
application of the information contained herein. The techniques
and suggestions are used at the reader's discretion and are not to
be considered a substitute for veterinary care. If you suspect a
medical problem consult your veterinarian.

T.F.H—The Leader in Responsible Animal Care for Over 50 Years!™
www.tfhpublications.com

# Contents

# Introduction

Knitting is something to be shared. Many of us will have knitted for our loved ones, often with varying degrees of appreciation, but who else shows us non-stop, unconditional love but our canine companions? So why should they be left out in the cold when everyone else in the family is wearing a lovingly knitted sweater?

This fantastic range of dog coats has been designed to reflect the many personalities and needs of our furry friends. You will find a dog coat to suit all occasions, be it a romp in the local park, a stroll on the beach or just an evening snooze by the fire. There are over 20 different designs included in the book. Perhaps your dog would be suited to Bright and Bobbly (see page 80) with its bold colors and texture – just the sweater for an outgoing, fun-loving hound. However, if your dog is the type to look down his nose at such frivolity, the Raingear for Rover (see page 28) or Frogged and Formal (see page 16) might be more to his or her taste. There are many more inspiring creations to choose from. So, whether you have a Classic Canine, a Funky Dawg or a Perfect Pooch, you are sure to find the coat to suit your four-legged friend. Enjoy your knitting!

# Choosing the size to knit

The patterns in this book are written for dogs with chest sizes from 16 in/41 cm to 28 in/72 cm, with the measurements shown in the table below. Dogs vary greatly in proportion, so these measurements should be used only as a guide. When choosing a size for your dog, use the chest measurement (measured just behind the forelegs) and the collar measurement to determine which size to knit.

The length of the coat that you choose to knit can easily be adjusted to suit your dog. You will see that the patterns for the blanket-type coats in this book also give a measurement for the width of the coat (edge to edge) – you may wish to check this before the chest size if your dog has particularly short legs. The strap on this style of coat is easily adjusted, in both length and position.

Dogs can be very inquisitive, so all finishing, buttons and embellishments should be made extra secure. No matter how well made a coat is, your dog should not be left wearing it unsupervised.

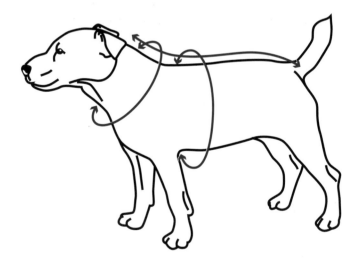

| Sizes | | | | | | | |
|---|---|---|---|---|---|---|---|
| XXS | XS | S | M | L | XL | XXL | |
| **Chest measurement** | | | | | | | |
| 16 | 18 | 20 | 22 | 24 | 26 | 28 | in |
| 41 | 46 | 51 | 56 | 61 | 67 | 72 | cm |
| **Collar size** | | | | | | | |
| 12 | 12½ | 13 | 13½ | 15 | 17 | 19 | in |
| 30 | 32 | 33 | 35 | 38 | 44 | 49 | cm |
| **Length from collar to tail** | | | | | | | |
| 13 | 14 | 16 | 18 | 20 | 23 | 24 | in |
| 33 | 36 | 41 | 46 | 51 | 59 | 61 | cm |

## Size abbreviations

The abbreviations for the dog coat sizes are as follows:

**XXS**    extra-extra small; to fit 16 in/41 cm chest
**XS**     extra small; to fit 18 in/46 cm chest
**S**      small; to fit 20 in/51 cm chest
**M**      medium; to fit 22 in/56 cm chest
**L**      large; to fit 24 in/61 cm chest
**XL**     extra large; to fit 26 in/67 cm chest
**XXL**    extra-extra large; to fit 28 in/72 cm chest

# Useful information

## Knitting abbreviations

The following are the general abbreviations used for knitting patterns. Special abbreviations, such as those for cable patterns, are given with the individual patterns.

**alt** alternate
**beg** begin(ning)
**cm** centimeter(s)
**cont** continu(e)(ing)
**dec** decreas(e)(ing)
**DK** double knitting (a medium-weight yarn)
**foll** follow(s)(ing)
**g** gram(s)
**in** inch(es)
**inc** increas(e)(ing); increase one st by working into front and back of st
**K** knit
**K2tog** knit next 2 sts together
**m** meter(s)
**M1** make one st; pick up strand between st just knit and next st with tip of left needle and work into back of it
**mm** millimeter(s)
**oz** ounce(s)
**P** purl
**P2tog** purl next 2 sts together
**patt** pattern; or work in pattern
**psso** pass slipped stitch over
**rem** remain(s)(ing)
**rev st st** reverse stocking/ stockinette st; purl RS rows and knit WS rows

**rep** repeat(s)(ing)
**RS** right side
**sl** slip
**st(s)** stitch(es)
**st st** stocking/stockinette stitch; knit RS rows and purl WS rows
**tbl** through back of loop(s)
**tog** together
**WS** wrong side
**yd** yard(s)
**yf** yarn forward; bring yarn forward between needles and over right needle to make a new st (US yarn over – yo)
**yrn** yarn round needle; wrap yarn around top of right needle from front to back and bring it to front again between needles to make a new st (US yarn over – yo)
* Repeat instructions after asterisk or between asterisks as many times as instructed.
[ ] Repeat instructions inside square brackets as many times as instructed.

## US and UK knitting terminology

A few knitting terms are different in the US and the UK. Where this occurs, they appear in the instructions divided by a / with the US term first and the UK term second.

| US | UK |
| --- | --- |
| bind off | cast off |
| seed stitch | moss stitch |
| snap | press-stud fastener |
| stockinette stitch | stocking stitch |
| duplicate stitch | Swiss darning |
| gauge | tension (size of stitch) |
| work even | work straight |
| yarn over (yo) | yarn forward (yf) |
| yarn over (yo) | yarn round needle (yrn) |

## Knitting needle conversion chart

This chart shows how the different knitting-needle-size systems compare for the needle sizes in this book. Where there is no exact match, the closest size is used as the equivalent. Always check your needle size by knitting a tension/gauge swatch before beginning a knitting project.

| US sizes | Metric | Old UK |
| --- | --- | --- |
| 2 | 2¾ mm | 12 |
| 3 | 3¼ mm | 10 |
| 6 | 4 mm | 8 |
| 7 | 4½ mm | 7 |
| 8 | 5 mm | 6 |
| 10½ | 7 mm | 2 |
| 11 | 8 mm | 0 |
| 15 | 10 mm | 000 |
| 17 | 12 mm | – |
| 19 | 15 mm | – |

# Classic canine

Some dogs have more refined tastes than others, and the designs in this section use simple stitch patterns and shaping to produce stylish, timeless coats suited to them. Creations such as Raingear for Rover or Lace-edged Lady are perfect for those four-legged friends who like to look their best at all times.

# 1 Textured sweater

The simplest of all textured stitches, moss/seed stitch is used here to create a snug sweater. Worked in a bright, chunky yarn, this cover-up doesn't even need buttonholes. Just cast on and your dog will soon be wrapped up warmly.

### Yarn
2 (2: 2: 2: 3: 3: 4) 3½ oz/100 g balls of Rowan *Spray* in mixed pink, orange and blue/Languid 00003

### Needles and extras
Pair each of US 11 (8 mm) and US 15 (10 mm) knitting needles
3 (3: 3: 3: 4: 4: 5) x 20 mm/¾ in diameter buttons

### Tension/Gauge
9 sts and 16 rows to 4 in/10 cm over moss/seed stitch using US 15 (10 mm) needles.

### Abbreviations
**dec2** (decrease 2) slip one stitch, work 2 stitches together, pass slipped stitch over.
See page 9 for other abbreviations.

### Sizes and measurements

| XXS | XS | S | M | L | XL | XXL | |
|-----|-----|-----|-----|-----|-----|-----|-----|

**To fit chest measuring approximately**

| XXS | XS | S | M | L | XL | XXL | |
|-----|-----|-----|-----|-----|-----|-----|-----|
| 16 | 18 | 20 | 22 | 24 | 26 | 28 | in |
| 41 | 46 | 51 | 56 | 61 | 67 | 72 | cm |

**Knitted measurements**
**Around chest**

| XXS | XS | S | M | L | XL | XXL | |
|-----|-----|-----|-----|-----|-----|-----|-----|
| 21½ | 23½ | 25 | 27½ | 30 | 32 | 33½ | in |
| 54.5 | 59 | 63 | 70 | 76.5 | 81 | 85.5 | cm |

**Length (from centre back neck edge, excluding collar)**

| XXS | XS | S | M | L | XL | XXL | |
|-----|-----|-----|-----|-----|-----|-----|-----|
| 7 | 7¾ | 9 | 11 | 13 | 14 | 15½ | in |
| 18 | 20 | 23 | 28 | 33 | 35 | 40 | cm |

## Sweater

Using US 11 (8 mm) needles, cast on 49 (53: 57: 63: 69: 73: 77) sts.

**Row 1** K1, *P1, K1, rep from * to end.

Last row is repeated to form moss/seed st patt.

Work 5 rows more in moss/seed st.

Change to US 15 (10 mm) needles.

Cont in moss/seed st until sweater measures 3 (4: 5: 6½: 7½: 8½: 10) in/8 (10: 13: 17: 19: 21: 26) cm/from cast-on edge, ending with a WS row.

**Divide for leg holes**

Keeping moss/seed st patt correct throughout, cont as foll:

**Next row (RS)** Patt 7 (9: 9: 9: 9: 11: 13), work 2tog, then turn, leaving rem sts on a holder.

Working on these 8 (10: 10: 10: 10: 12: 14) sts only, cont as foll:

Work 1 row.

**Next row (RS)** Patt to last 2 sts, work 2tog. 7 (9: 9: 9: 9: 11: 13) sts.

Work 5 (5: 5: 5: 9: 9: 9) rows more.

Place these sts on another holder and DO NOT break off yarn but set this ball aside to use later.

With RS facing, join a new ball of yarn at first leg divide on first holder and, keeping patt correct throughout, work 2tog, patt 5 (5: 7: 9: 13: 13: 13), work 2tog, then turn, leaving rem sts on the holder. 7 (7: 9: 11: 15: 15: 15) sts.

Work 1 row.

**Next row (WS)** Work 2tog, patt to last 2 sts, work 2tog. 5 (5: 7: 9: 13: 13: 13) sts.

Work 3 rows.

**Next row** Work 2tog, patt to last 2 sts, work 2tog. 3 (3: 5: 7: 11: 11: 11) sts.

**Sizes L, XL and XXL only:**

Rep last 4 rows once more. 9 (9: 9) sts.

**All sizes:**

Work 1 row.

Break off yarn and place these sts on another holder.

With RS facing, rejoin yarn to rem sts on first holder and, keeping patt correct throughout, work 2tog, patt to end. 30 (32: 34: 38: 40: 42: 44) sts.

Work 1 row.

**Next row (RS)** Work 2tog, patt to end. 29 (31: 33: 37: 39: 41: 43) sts.

Work 5 (5: 5: 5: 9: 9: 9) rows more in moss/seed st.

### Join sections

Slide all sts on to one needle and with RS facing, using ball of yarn set aside previously and keeping moss/seed st patt correct throughout, cont as foll:

**Next row (RS)** Patt across all sts. 39 (43: 47: 53: 57: 61: 65) sts.

Work 1 row.

**Next row** Patt 3 (5: 7: 5: 5: 5: 5) sts, [dec2, patt 4 (4: 4: 8: 8: 8: 8)] twice, dec2, patt to end. 33 (37: 41: 47: 51: 55: 59) sts.

Work 1 row.

**Next row** Patt 2 (4: 6: 4: 4: 4: 4) sts, [dec2, patt 2 (2: 2: 6: 6: 6: 6)] twice, dec2, patt to end. 27 (31: 35: 41: 45: 49: 53) sts.

**Sizes M, L, XL and XXL only:**

Work 1 row.

**Next row (RS)** Patt 3, [dec2, patt 4] twice, dec2, patt to end. 35 (39: 43: 47) sts.

**All sizes:**

Work 3 rows.

Cast/bind off in moss/seed st.

### Collar

Using US 11 (8 mm) needles, cast on 31 (33: 37: 45: 55: 59: 63) sts.

**Row 1 (RS)** *K1, P1, rep from * to last st, K1.

Last row is repeated to form moss/seed st patt.

Work 1 row more in moss/seed st.

**Next row** K1, P1, K1, P3tog, work in moss/seed st to last 6 sts, P3tog, K1, P1, K1. 27 (29: 33: 41: 51: 55: 59) sts.

Work 3 rows more in moss/seed st.

Rep last 4 rows 1 (1: 1: 1: 2: 2: 2) times more. 23 (25: 29: 37: 43: 47: 51) sts.

Cast/bind off in moss/seed st.

### To finish

Do not press.

Sew collar on to sweater. Using the photograph as a guide, sew on buttons equally spaced along one edge of sweater. To fasten sweater, push buttons through fabric of opposite edge.

Frogged and formal

Watch your dog step out with his nose in the air when he is wearing this gold-trimmed jacket. Worked in a soft, warm yarn and finished with a classic gold trim, it is simple yet stylish.

**Yarn**
2 (3: 3: 4: 5: 5: 6) 1¾ oz/50 g balls of Rowan *Kid Classic* in main shade **A** (dark red/Cherry Red 847) and one 1 oz/25 g ball of Rowan *Lurex Shimmer* in **B** (gold/Antique White Gold 332)

**Needles and extras**
Pair of US 8 (5 mm) knitting needles
Two US 3 (3¼ mm) double-pointed needles
1 x ½ in/12 mm diameter gold knot button
2 press-stud fasteners/snaps

**Tension/Gauge**
19 sts and 25 rows to 4 in/10 cm over stocking/stockinette stitch using US 8 (5 mm) needles.

**Abbreviations**
See page 9 for abbreviations.

**Sizes and measurements**

| XXS | XS | S | M | L | XL | XXL | |
|-----|-----|-----|-----|-----|-----|-----|-----|

**To fit chest measuring approximately**

| XXS | XS | S | M | L | XL | XXL | |
|-----|-----|-----|-----|-----|-----|-----|-----|
| 16 | 18 | 20 | 22 | 24 | 26 | 28 | in |
| 41 | 46 | 51 | 56 | 61 | 67 | 72 | cm |

**Knitted measurements**
**Width across dog's back (excluding edging and strap)**

| 12¾ | 14 | 15½ | 16½ | 17½ | 19 | 20 | in |
|-----|-----|-----|-----|-----|-----|-----|-----|
| 32.5 | 36 | 39 | 42 | 45 | 48.5 | 51.5 | cm |

**Length (from center back neck edge, excluding edging)**

| 10 | 11 | 13 | 15 | 17 | 20 | 21½ | in |
|-----|-----|-----|-----|-----|-----|-----|-----|
| 25.5 | 28 | 33 | 38 | 43.5 | 51 | 54 | cm |

## Coat

Using US 8 (5 mm) needles and A, cast on 62 (68: 74: 80: 86: 92: 98) sts.

Work 3 rows in garter st (knit every row).

**Patt row 1 (WS)** K2, P to last 2 sts, K2.

**Patt row 2** K to end.

Last 2 rows are repeated to form patt (st st with 2-st garter st borders).

Cont in patt until coat measures 10 (11: 13: 15: 17: 20: 21½) in/25.5 (28: 33: 38: 43.5: 51: 54) cm from cast-on edge, ending with a WS row.

### Shape neck

Keeping patt correct throughout, cont as foll:

**Next row (RS)** Patt 27 (29: 31: 33: 35: 37: 39), then turn, leaving rem sts on a holder.

Cast/bind off 3 sts at beg of next row. 24 (26: 28: 30: 32: 34: 36) sts.

Dec 1 st at neck edge on next 3 rows. 21 (23: 25: 27: 29: 31: 33) sts.

Work 1 row.

Dec 1 st at neck edge of next row and foll 2 alt rows. 18 (20: 22: 24: 26: 28: 30) sts.

Work straight/even until coat measures 14 (15½: 17½: 19½: 21½: 25½: 27½) in/36 (39: 44: 49: 54: 65: 70) cm from cast-on edge, ending with a WS row.

Work 3 rows in garter st.

Cast/bind off.

With RS facing, rejoin A to rem sts and, keeping patt correct throughout, cast/bind off 8 (10: 12: 14: 16: 18: 20) sts, knit to end. 27 (29: 31: 33: 35: 37: 39) sts.

**Next row (WS)** K2, P to last 2 sts, P2tog. 26 (28: 30: 32: 34: 36: 38) sts.

Cast/bind off 2 sts at beg of next row. 24 (26: 28: 30: 32: 34: 36) sts.

Dec 1 st at neck edge of next 4 rows. 20 (22: 24: 26: 28: 30: 32) sts.

Work 1 row.

Dec 1 st at neck edge of next row and foll alt row. 18 (20: 22: 24: 26: 28: 30) sts.

Work straight/even until coat measures 14 (15½: 17½: 19½: 21½: 25½: 27½) in/36 (39: 44: 49: 54: 65: 70) cm from cast-on edge, ending with a WS row.

Work 3 rows in garter st.

Cast/bind off.

## Strap

Using US 8 (5 mm) needles and A, cast on 10 (10: 10: 12: 12: 14: 14) sts.

Work 3 rows in garter st.

**Patt row 1 (WS)** K2, P to last 2 sts, K2.

**Patt row 2** K to end.

Last 2 rows are repeated to form patt (st st with 2-st garter st borders).

Cont in patt until strap measures 12 (13: 14½: 15½: 17: 18: 19½) in/30 (33: 37: 39.5: 43.5: 46: 50) cm from cast-on edge, ending with a WS row.

Work 3 rows in garter st.

Cast/bind off.

## Edging

Using US 3 (3¼ mm) double-pointed needles and B, cast on 4 sts.

**Row 1** K4, do not turn work but slide sts to opposite end of needle and place this needle in left hand ready to beg next row.

Rep last row until edging measures 56 (58: 61: 63: 66: 73: 78) in/143 (148.5: 156: 161: 167: 187: 199) cm from cast-on edge.

Leave sts on needle and DO NOT break off yarn.

## To finish

Press coat lightly on WS following instructions on yarn label and avoiding garter stitch.

Starting at right front neck edge and using the photograph as a guide, slip stitch edging in place around edge of coat, forming frogging and a loop at center front for button and forming a loop at each back corner. (If necessary, work more rows on edging or unravel rows until edging fits as required.) Cast/bind off edging sts and sew ends together.

Sew on button to correspond with button loop. Sew cast-on edge of strap to inside of coat so that it will sit just behind the foreleg. Sew one press-stud fastener/snap to each free corner of strap and to corresponding position on the inside of coat.

# 3 Button-up sweater

Chill winter breezes won't bother your best friend when he is wearing this button-up sweater. Worked in classic cream, it will complement any color of fur. Use your choice of buttons to add a personal touch.

**Yarn**
3 (4: 5: 6: 9) 1¾ oz/50 g balls of Rowan *All Seasons Cotton* in cream/Organic 178

**Needles and extras**
Pair each of US 7 (4½ mm) and US 8 (5 mm) knitting needles
5 (7: 9: 9: 12) x ¾ in diameter buttons

**Gauge/Tension**
24 sts and 25 rows to 4 in/10 cm over rib pattern using US 8 (5 mm) needles.

**Abbreviations**
See page 9 for abbreviations.

**Sizes and measurements**

| XXS | XS | S | M | XL | |
|-----|-----|-----|-----|-----|-----|

**To fit chest measuring approximately**

| XXS | XS | S | M | XL | |
|-----|-----|-----|-----|-----|-----|
| 16 | 17½ | 20 | 22 | 26 | in |
| 41 | 44 | 51 | 56 | 67 | cm |

**Knitted measurements**
**Around chest**

| XXS | XS | S | M | XL | |
|-----|-----|-----|-----|-----|-----|
| 16 | 17½ | 20 | 22 | 26 | in |
| 41 | 44 | 51 | 56 | 67.5 | cm |

**Approximate length (from center back neck edge, excluding collar)**

| XXS | XS | S | M | XL | |
|-----|-----|-----|-----|-----|-----|
| 9 | 10 | 12 | 13½ | 17½ | in |
| 23.5 | 24.5 | 30.5 | 34.5 | 44 | cm |

## Sweater

Using US 7 (4½ mm) needles, cast on 98 (106: 122: 134: 162) sts.

**Rib row 1 (RS)** P2, *K2, P2, rep from * to end.
**Rib row 2** K2, *P2, K2, rep from * to end.
Change to US 8 (5 mm) needles.

**Patt row 1 (buttonhole row) (RS)** *P2, K2, rep from * to last 6 sts, P1, P2tog, yrn/yo twice, P2tog, P1.
**Patt row 2** K2, [P1, K1] into double yrn/yo, K2, *P2, K2, rep from * to end.
**Patt row 3** P2, *K2, P2, rep from * to end.
**Patt row 4** K2, *P2, K2, rep from * to end.
**Patt rows 5–10** Rep rows 3 and 4 three times.
Last 10 rows are repeated to form rib and buttonhole patt.
Work in rib and buttonhole patt until sweater measures approximately 5½ (5½: 7: 8½: 12) in/13.5 (13.5: 17.5: 21.5: 29.5) cm from cast-on edge, ending with a patt row 2.

### Divide for leg holes

### Left side

Keeping patt correct throughout, cont as foll:

**Next row (RS)** Patt 25 (25: 29: 33: 41), K2tog, K1, then turn, leaving rem sts on a holder.
Working on these 27 (27: 31: 35: 43) sts only, cont as foll:
**Next row** P1, P2tog, *P2, K2, rep from * to end.
26 (26: 30: 34: 42) sts.

**Next row** Cast/bind off 2 sts, patt to last 3 sts, K2tog, K1. 23 (23: 27: 31: 39) sts.
**Next row** P1, P2tog, patt to last 2 sts, P2tog. 21 (21: 25: 29: 37) sts.
**Next row** Cast/bind off 3 sts, patt to end. 18 (18: 22: 26: 34) sts.
Work 4 (6: 8: 8: 10) rows in patt, dec 1 st at beg of 2nd and 4th of these rows. 16 (16: 20: 24: 32) sts.
**Next row** P2, M1, patt to end. 17 (17: 21: 25: 33) sts.
**Next row** Patt to last 3 sts, K1 M1, K2. 18 (18: 22: 26: 34) sts.
**Next row** P2, M1, patt to end. 19 (19: 23: 27: 35) sts.
Place these sts on another holder and DO NOT break off yarn but set this ball aside to use later.

### Chest section

With RS facing, rejoin yarn to rem sts and cast/bind off 2 sts, K2tog tbl, P1, [K2, P2] 2 (4: 6: 7: 8) times, K2, P1, K2tog, K1, then turn, leaving rem sts on holder.
Working on these 16 (24: 32: 36: 40) sts only and keeping patt correct throughout, cont as foll:
**Next row (WS)** P1, P2tog, patt to last 3 sts, P2tog tbl, P1. 14 (22: 30: 34: 38) sts.
**Next row** K1, K2tog tbl, patt to last 3 sts, K2tog, K1. 12 (20: 28: 32: 36) sts.
Rep first of last 2 rows once more. 10 (18: 26: 30: 34) sts.

Work 5 (7: 9: 9: 11) rows in patt.

**Next row** P2, M1, patt to last 2 sts, M1, P2. 12 (20: 28: 32: 36) sts.

**Next row** K2, M1, patt to last 2 sts, M1, K2. 14 (22: 30: 34: 38) sts.

Rep first of last 2 rows once more. 16 (24: 32: 36: 40) sts.
Break off yarn and place these sts on a holder.

### Right side

With RS facing, rejoin yarn to rem sts and cast/bind off 2 sts, K2tog tbl, P1, [K2, P2] 6 (6: 7: 8: 10) times, K1, then turn, leaving rem sts on holder.

Working on these 28 (28: 32: 36: 44) sts only and, keeping patt correct throughout, cont as foll:

**Next row (WS)** Cast/bind off 3 sts, patt to last 3 sts, P2tog tbl, P1. 24 (24: 28: 32: 40) sts.

**Next row** K1, K2tog tbl, patt to last 2 sts, K2tog. 22 (22: 26: 30: 38) sts.

Rep first of last 2 rows once more. 18 (18: 22: 26: 34) sts.
Work 5 (7: 9: 9: 11) rows in patt, dec 1 st at beg of 2nd and 4th of these rows. 16 (16: 20: 24: 32) sts.

**Next row** Patt to last 3 sts, M1, P2. 17 (17: 21: 25: 33) sts.

**Next row** K2, M1, patt to end. 18 (18: 22: 26: 34) sts.

Rep first of last 2 rows once more. 19 (19: 23: 27: 35) sts.
Break off yarn and leave rem sts on a holder.

### Buttonband overlap

With RS facing, rejoin yarn to rem sts and, keeping patt correct throughout, cast/bind off 12 (12: 12: 12: 20) sts, patt to end. 7 (7: 7: 7: 7) sts.

Dec 1 st at end of next row. 6 (6: 6: 6: 6) sts.

Cast/bind off 3 sts at beg of next row. 3 (3: 3: 3: 3) sts.

Dec 1 st at end of next row.

Cast/bind off 2 rem sts.

### Join sections

With RS facing, using ball of yarn previously set aside and keeping patt correct throughout, patt across 17 (17: 21: 25: 33) sts, M1, K2 from 1st holder, cast on 2 sts, K2, M1, patt across 12 (20: 28: 32: 36) sts, M1, K2 from 2nd holder, cast on 2 sts, K2, M1, patt across rem 17 (17: 21: 25: 33) sts from 3rd holder. 62 (70: 86: 98: 118) sts.

Work 1 (3: 5: 5: 7) rows in patt, so ending with a WS row.

### Shape front

Place marker at center of row between 2 center sts.

**Next row (RS)** Patt to 2 sts before marker, K2tog tbl, K2tog, patt to end. 60 (68: 84: 96: 116) sts.

**Next row** Patt to 2 sts before marker, P2tog, P2tog tbl, patt to end. 58 (66: 82: 94: 114) sts.

Rep last 2 rows 2 times more. 50 (58: 74: 86: 106) sts.

**Next row** Patt to 4 sts before marker, [K2tog, K2tog tbl] twice, patt to end. 46 (54: 70: 82: 102) sts.

**Next row** Patt to 4 sts before marker, [P2tog tbl, P2tog] twice, patt to end. 42 (50: 66: 78: 98) sts.

Rep last 2 rows once more. 34 (42: 58: 70: 90) sts.

### Left front

**Next row** Patt to marker, then turn, leaving rem sts on a holder.

Working on these 17 (21: 29: 35: 45) sts only, cont as foll:
Cast/bind off 3 (4: 9: 9: 10) sts at beg of next row.
Cast/bind off rem 14 (17: 20: 26: 35) sts.

### Right front

With RS facing, rejoin yarn to rem sts and cont as foll:
Cast/bind off 3 (4: 9: 9: 10) sts at beg of next row.
Cast/bind off rem 14 (17: 20: 26: 35) sts.

## Collar

Sew front seam.

With RS facing and using US 8 (5 mm) needles, pick up and knit 30 (32: 36: 40: 48) sts down left side of neck, 30 (32: 36: 40: 48) sts up right side of neck, 12 (12: 12: 12: 20) sts across back neck, and 6 sts down overlap. 78 (82: 90: 98: 122) sts.

**Rib row 1 (WS)** K2, *P2, K2, rep from * to end.

**Rib row 2** P2, *K2, P2, rep from * to end.

Last 2 rows are repeated to form rib patt.

Work 1 row more in rib patt.

**Buttonhole row** P2, K2tog tbl, yf/yo twice, K2tog, patt to end.

**Next row** Patt to last 4 sts, [P1, K1] into double yf/yo, K2.

Cont in rib patt, working a buttonhole row on every 10th row, until collar measures approximately 4 (6½: 8½: 10: 12) in/10 (17: 21: 26: 30) cm, ending with one row after a buttonhole row.

Cast/bind off in patt.

## To finish

Do not press.

Sew on the buttons to correspond with the buttonholes, making sure buttons are correctly positioned on collar for turn-back.

# 4 Lace-edged lady

For a touch of canine class, why not create this simple yet elegant coat? Edged with a contrasting mauve lace border, this is perfect for the discerning, genteel dog who likes to be seen at her best.

**Yarn**
2 (2: 2: 3: 3: 4: 5) 1¾ oz/50 g balls of Rowan *4 ply Soft* in main shade **A** (light green/Goblin 379) and 2 (2: 2: 2: 3: 3: 3) balls in **B** (mauve/Day Dream 378)

**Needles and extras**
Pair of US 3 (3¼ mm) knitting needles
3 hook-and-eye fasteners
2 press-stud fasteners/snaps

**Tension/Gauge**
28 sts and 36 rows to 4 in/10 cm over stocking/ stockinette stitch using US 3 (3¼ mm) needles.

**Abbreviations**
See page 9 for abbreviations.

**Sizes and measurements**

| XXS | XS | S | M | L | XL | XXL | |
|---|---|---|---|---|---|---|---|

**To fit chest measuring approximately**

| XXS | XS | S | M | L | XL | XXL | |
|---|---|---|---|---|---|---|---|
| 16 | 18 | 20 | 22 | 24 | 26 | 28 | in |
| 41 | 46 | 51 | 56 | 61 | 67 | 72 | cm |

**Knitted measurements**
**Width (excluding laced edging and strap)**

| XXS | XS | S | M | L | XL | XXL | |
|---|---|---|---|---|---|---|---|
| 12½ | 13½ | 14 | 15 | 16½ | 17½ | 18½ | in |
| 31.5 | 33.5 | 35.5 | 38 | 42 | 44.5 | 47 | cm |

**Length (from center back neck edge, excluding lace edging)**

| XXS | XS | S | M | L | XL | XXL | |
|---|---|---|---|---|---|---|---|
| 11 | 12 | 14 | 15½ | 18 | 21½ | 22 | in |
| 28 | 30.5 | 35.5 | 40 | 46 | 54.5 | 56 | cm |

## Coat

Using US 3 (3¼ mm) needles and A, cast on 72 (78: 84: 90: 102: 108: 116) sts.

**Row 1** K to end.

**Row 2** Cast on 3 sts, P to end. 75 (81: 87: 93: 105: 111: 119) sts.

**Row 3** Cast on 3 sts, K to end. 78 (84: 90: 96: 108: 114: 122) sts.

**Row 4** P2, M1, P to last 2 sts, M1, P2. 80 (86: 92: 98: 110: 116: 124) sts.

**Row 5** K2, M1, K to last 2 sts, M1, K2. 82 (88: 94: 100: 112: 118: 126) sts.

**Row 6** P to end.

**Row 7** Rep row 5. 84 (90: 96: 102: 114: 120: 128) sts.

**Row 8** P to end.

**Row 9** Rep row 5. 86 (92: 98: 104: 116: 122: 130) sts.

**Rows 10–12** Beg with a P row, work 3 rows in st st.

**Row 13** Rep row 5. 88 (94: 100: 106: 118: 124: 132) sts.

Beg with a P row, work straight/even in st st until coat measures 11 (12: 14: 15½: 18: 21½: 22) in/28 (30.5: 35.5: 40: 46: 54.5: 56) cm from cast-on edge, ending with a WS row.

### Shape neck

Working in st st throughout, cont as foll:

**Next row (RS)** K39 (41: 44: 47: 49: 51: 51), then turn, leaving rem sts on a holder.

Cast/bind off 3 sts at beg of next row. 36 (38: 41: 44: 46: 48: 48) sts.

Dec 1 st at neck edge of next 3 rows. 33 (35: 38: 41: 43: 45: 45) sts.

Work 1 row.

Dec 1 st at neck edge of next row and foll 2 alt rows. 30 (32: 35: 38: 40: 42: 42) sts.

Work 3 rows.

Dec 1 st a neck edge of next row and foll 4th row. 28 (30: 33: 36: 38: 40: 40) sts.

Work straight/even until coat measures 15 (16: 18: 19½: 23: 27: 28½) in/38 (40.5: 45.5: 50: 59: 68.5: 72) cm from cast-on edge, ending with a WS row.

**Next row (RS)** K2, K2tog, K to last 4 sts, K2tog tbl, K2. 26 (28: 31: 34: 36: 38: 38) sts.

Work 1 row.

**Next row** K2, K2tog, K to last 4 sts, K2tog tbl, K2. 24 (26: 29: 32: 34: 36: 36) sts.

Work 1 row.

**Next row** K2, K3tog, K to last 5 sts, K3tog tbl, K2. 20 (22: 25: 28: 30: 32: 32) sts.

Cast/bind off on WS.

With RS facing, rejoin yarn to rem sts and cont in st st throughout, cast/bind off 10 (12: 12: 12: 20: 22: 30) sts, knit to end. 39 (41: 44: 47: 49: 51: 51) sts.

**Next row (WS)** P to last 2 sts, P2tog. 38 (40: 43: 46: 48: 50: 50) sts.

Cast/bind off 2 sts at beg of next row. 36 (38: 41: 44: 46: 48: 48) sts.

Dec 1 st at neck edge of next 3 rows. 33 (35: 38: 41: 43: 45: 45) sts.

Work 1 row.

Dec 1 st at neck edge of next row and foll 2 alt rows. 30 (32: 35: 38: 40: 42: 42) sts.

Work 3 rows.

Dec 1 st a neck edge of next row and foll 4th row. 28 (30: 33: 36: 38: 40: 40) sts.

Work straight/even until coat measures 15 (16: 18: 19½: 23: 27: 28½) in/38 (40.5: 45.5: 50: 59: 68.5: 72) cm from cast-on edge, ending with a WS row.

**Next row (RS)** K2, K2tog, K to last 4 sts, K2tog tbl, K2. 26 (28: 31: 34: 36: 38: 38) sts.

Work 1 row.

**Next row** K2, K2tog, K to last 4 sts, K2tog tbl, K2. 24 (26: 29: 32: 34: 36: 36) sts.

Work 1 row.

**Next row** K2, K3tog, K to last 5 sts, K3tog tbl, K2. 20 (22: 25: 28: 30: 32: 32) sts.

Cast/bind off on WS.

## Strap

Using US 3 (3¼ mm) needles and B, cast on 11 (11: 15: 15: 21: 21: 21) sts.

**Row 1** *K1, P1, rep from * to end.

Last row is repeated to form moss/seed st patt.

Cont in moss/seed st until strap measures 7¾ (8½: 10½: 12½: 13: 13¼: 14) in/20 (22: 27: 32: 33: 34: 36) cm, ending with a WS row.

Cast/bind off in patt.

## Lace edging

Using US 3 (3¼ mm) needles and B, cast on 9 sts.

**Row 1 and every foll alt row** K to end.

**Row 2** K3, [K2tog, yf] twice, K1, yf, K1. 10 sts.

**Row 4** K2, [K2tog, yf] twice, K3, yf, K1. 11 sts.

**Row 6** K1, [K2tog, yf] twice, K5, yf, K1. 12 sts.

**Row 8** K3, [yf, K2tog] twice, K1, K2tog, yf, K2tog. 11 sts.

**Row 10** K4, yf, K2tog, yf, K3tog, yf, K2tog. 10 sts.

**Row 12** K5, yf, K3tog, yf, K2tog. 9 sts.

Last 12 rows are repeated to form lace patt.

Cont in lace patt until edging fits around entire edge of coat, ending with a row 12. Leave stitches on needle and DO NOT break off yarn.

## To finish

Press coat and lace edging lightly on WS, following instructions on yarn label.

Starting at right front neck corner, slip stitch edging in place around edge of coat, easing in fullness around corners (if necessary, work more rows on edging or unravel rows until edging fits as required). Cast/bind off edging sts and sew together cast-on and cast-/bound-off ends.

Sew hook-and-eye fasteners to center front edge, behind the lace.

Sew cast-on edge of strap to inside of coat so that it will sit just behind the foreleg. Sew press-stud fasteners/snaps to cast-/bound-off edge of strap and to inside of coat to correspond.

# 5 Raingear for Rover

Worked in a thick, hard-wearing cotton yarn, this is a classic-style coat for a smart, proud pet. The buckles make the chest straps and belt easy to adjust for the perfect fit.

**Yarn**
4 (4: 5: 5: 6: 7: 7) 1¾ oz/50 g balls of Rowan *Handknit Cotton* in taupe/Linen 205

**Needles and extras**
Pair each of US 6 (4 mm) and US 7 (4½ mm) knitting needles
2 (2: 2: 3: 3: 3: 3) 2 in/5 cm buckles

**Tension/Gauge**
19 sts and 28 rows to 14 in/10 cm over stocking/stockinette stitch using US 7 (4½ mm) needles.

## Abbreviations

**Kfb** = knit into front and back of st to increase one st.
**Pfb** = purl into front and back of st to increase one st.
**sl 1p** = slip one stitch purlwise from left needle on to right needle.
See page 9 for other abbreviations.

## Sizes and measurements

| | XXS | XS | S | M | L | XL | XXL | |
|---|---|---|---|---|---|---|---|---|
| **To fit chest measuring approximately** | | | | | | | | |
| | 16 | 18 | 20 | 22 | 24 | 26 | 28 | in |
| | 41 | 46 | 51 | 56 | 61 | 67 | 72 | cm |

**Knitted measurements**
**Width across back (excluding straps)**

| XXS | XS | S | M | L | XL | XXL | |
|---|---|---|---|---|---|---|---|
| 12½ | 13¼ | 14 | 15½ | 16 | 17½ | 20 | in |
| 31.5 | 34 | 36 | 40 | 41 | 44 | 51.5 | cm |

**Length (from center back neck edge, excluding collar)**

| XXS | XS | S | M | L | XL | XXL | |
|---|---|---|---|---|---|---|---|
| 8 | 8½ | 10½ | 12½ | 14 | 15 | 15½ | in |
| 20 | 22 | 27 | 32 | 36 | 38 | 40 | cm |

## Coat

Using US 7 (4½ mm) needles, cast on 48 (52: 56: 62: 66: 72: 86) sts.

**Row 1 (RS)** Kfb, K to last st, Kfb. 50 (54: 58: 64: 68: 74: 88) sts.

**Row 2** Pfb, P to last st, Pfb. 52 (56: 60: 66: 70: 76: 90) sts.

**Rows 3–6** Rep rows 1 and 2 twice. 60 (64: 68: 74: 78: 84: 98) sts.

**Row 7 (fold line) (RS)** P to end.

**Row 8** Rep row 2. 62 (66: 70: 76: 80: 86: 100) sts.

**Row 9** Rep row 1. 64 (68: 72: 78: 82: 88: 102) sts.

**Row 10** Pfb, P2, sl 1p, P to last 4 sts, sl 1p, P2, Pfb. 66 (70: 74: 80: 84: 90: 104) sts. (Slipped sts form hem fold lines.)

**Row 11** Rep row 1. 68 (72: 76: 82: 86: 92: 106) sts.

**Row 12** Pfb, P3, sl 1p, P to last 5 sts, sl 1p, P3, Pfb. 70 (74: 78: 84: 88: 94: 108) sts.

**Row 13** Rep row 1. 72 (76: 80: 86: 90: 96: 110) sts.

**Row 14** P6, sl 1p, P to last 7 sts, sl 1p, P6.

**Row 15** K to end.

Rows 14 and 15 are repeated to form patt.

Cont straight/even in patt until coat measures 8 (8½: 10½: 12½: 14: 15: 15½) in/20 (22: 27: 32: 36: 38: 40) cm from fold line, ending with a WS row.

## Shape neck

Keeping patt correct throughout, cont as foll:

**Next row (RS)** Patt 32 (34: 36: 39: 41: 43: 50), then turn, leaving rem sts on a holder.

Cast/bind off 3 sts at beg of next row. 29 (31: 33: 36: 38: 40: 47) sts.

Dec 1 st at neck edge of next 5 rows. 24 (26: 28: 31: 33: 35: 42) sts.

Work straight/even until coat measures 13½ (14: 17½: 19½: 21½: 24: 25½) in/34 (36: 45: 50: 55: 61: 65) cm from fold line, ending with WS row.

**Next row (RS)** K2tog, K to end. 23 (25: 27: 30: 32: 34: 41) sts.

**Next row** P to last 6 sts, sl 1p, P3, P2tog. 22 (24: 26: 29: 31: 33: 40) sts.

**Next row** K2tog, K to end. 21 (23: 25: 28: 30: 32: 39) sts.

**Next row** P to last 4 sts, sl 1p, P1, P2tog. 20 (22: 24: 27: 29: 31: 38) sts.

**Next row** K2tog, K to end. 19 (21: 23: 26: 28: 30: 37) sts.

**Next row** P to last 2 sts, P2tog. 18 (20: 22: 25: 27: 29: 36) sts.

**Next row (fold line) (RS)** P to end.

**Next row** P to last 2 sts, P2tog. 17 (19: 21: 24: 26: 28: 35) sts.

**Next row** K2tog, K to end. 16 (18: 20: 23: 25: 27: 34) sts.

Rep last 2 rows twice more. 12 (14: 16: 19: 21: 23: 30) sts. Cast/bind off on WS.

With RS facing, rejoin yarn to rem sts and, keeping patt correct throughout, cast/bind off 8 (8: 8: 8: 8: 10: 10) sts, patt to end. 32 (34: 36: 39: 41: 43: 50) sts.

**Next row** Patt to last 2 sts, P2tog. 31 (33: 35: 38: 40: 42: 49) sts.

Cast/bind off 2 sts at beg of next row. 29 (31: 33: 36: 38: 40: 47) sts.

Dec 1 st at neck edge of next 5 rows. 24 (26: 28: 31: 33: 35: 42) sts.

Work straight/even until coat measures 13½ (14: 17½: 19½: 21½: 24: 25½) in/34 (36: 45: 50: 55: 61: 65) cm from fold line, ending with a WS row.

**Next row (RS)** K to last 2 sts, K2tog. 23 (25: 27: 30: 32: 34: 41) sts.

**Next row** P2tog, P3, sl 1p, P to end. 22 (24: 26: 29: 31: 33: 40) sts.

**Next row** K to last 2 sts, K2tog. 21 (23: 25: 28: 30: 32: 39) sts.

**Next row** P2tog, P1, sl 1p, P to end. 20 (22: 24: 27: 29: 31: 38) sts.

**Next row** K to last 2 sts, K2tog. 19 (21: 23: 26: 28: 30: 37) sts.

**Next row** P2tog, P to end. 18 (20: 22: 25: 27: 29: 36) sts.

**Next row (fold line) (RS)** P to end.

**Next row** P2tog, P to end. 17 (19: 21: 24: 26: 28: 35) sts.

**Next row** K to last 2 sts, K2tog. 16 (18: 20: 23: 25: 27: 34) sts.

Rep last 2 rows twice more 12 (14: 16: 19: 21: 23: 30) sts. Cast/bind off on WS.

## Collar

Using US 6 (4 mm) needles, cast on 83 (87: 103: 107: 111: 137: 145) sts.

**Row 1 (RS)** *K1, P1, rep from * to last st, K1.

Last row is repeated to form moss/seed st patt.

Work 3 rows more in moss/seed st.

**Next row (RS)** K1, P1, K1, P3tog, work in moss/seed st to last 6 sts, P3tog, K1, P1, K1. 79 (83: 99: 103: 107: 133: 141) sts.

Work 3 rows more in moss/seed st.

Rep last 4 rows 3 (4: 4: 5: 5: 7: 7) times more. 67 (67: 83: 83: 87: 105: 113) sts.

Cast/bind off in moss/seed st.

## Main belt

Using US 6 (4 mm) needles, cast on 9 sts.

Work in moss/seed st as for collar until belt measures 18½ (22½: 24: 26: 29: 31: 33½) in/47 (57: 61.5: 66.5: 74: 79: 85) cm from cast-on edge, ending with a WS row.

**Shape end**

**Keeping moss/seed st patt correct throughout, cont as foll:

**Next row** Patt 3, work 3tog, patt 3. 7 sts.

**Next row** Patt to end.

**Next row** Patt 2, work 3tog, patt 2. 5 sts.

**Next row** Patt to end.

**Next row** Patt 1, work 3tog, patt 1. 3 sts.

**Next row** Work 3tog.

Fasten off.**

### Front strap

Using US 6 (4 mm) needles, cast on 9 sts.
Work in moss/seed st as for collar until strap measures
4 in/10 cm from cast-on edge, ending with a WS row.
Rep from ** to ** to shape end as for main belt.
Make 0 (0: 0: 1: 1: 1: 1) more front strap in same way.

### Front buckle section

Using US 6 (4 mm) needles cast on 9 sts.
Work in moss/seed st as for collar until front buckle
section measures 4 in/10 cm from cast-on edge.
Cast/bind off in moss/seed st.
Make 0 (0: 0: 1: 1: 1: 1) more front buckle section in the
same way.

### Belt loops (make 2)

Using US 6 (4 mm) needles, cast on 12 sts.
Beg with a K row, work 3 rows in st st.
Knit 1 row (fold line).
Beg with a K row, work 7 rows in st st.
Knit 1 row (fold line).
Beg with a K row, work 3 rows in st st.
Cast/bind off on WS.

### To finish

Fold all hems to WS and slip stitch in place.
Press the coat lightly on WS, following instructions on
yarn label.
Sew cast-/bound-off edge of collar to neck edge. Fold belt
loops along fold lines and stitch cast-on edge to cast-
/bound-off edge. Fold coat in half lengthways, then
position one belt loop halfway up each side and sew ends
of belt loops to coat. Fold cast-on end of main belt around
the center of a buckle and sew in place. Repeat this
process with front buckle sections. Sew buckle end of
main belt to center back of coat, aligning strap with belt
loops. Using the photograph as a guide, sew front buckle
and front straps to front of coat.

33

# 6 Fabulous and felted

Knitted and then felted, this virtually windproof coat is ideal for those
long winter walks. There is a choice of a plain or a striped version,
both finished with a smart, blanket-stitch edging.

## Yarn
**Plain version**
3 (3: 4: 5: 5: 7: 8) 1¾ oz/50 g balls of Rowan *Kid
Classic* in main shade **A** (purple/Royal 835) and one
ball in **B** (pale blue/Iced Jade 848)
**Striped version**
3 (3: 3: 4: 4: 6: 6) 1¾ oz/50 g balls of Rowan *Kid
Classic* in main shade **A** (brown/Peat 832), one ball
of **B** (red/Cherry Red 847), one ball of **C** (orange/
Sandalwood 849) and 1 (1: 1: 1: 1: 2: 2) balls of
**D** (dark red/Crushed Velvet 825)

## Needles and extras
Pair of US 8 (5 mm) knitting needles
4 x ¾ in/20 mm diameter buttons

## Tension/Gauge
19 sts and 25 rows to 10 cm/4 in over stocking/
stockinette stitch *before felting* using US 8
(5 mm) needles.

## Sizes and measurements

| | XXS | XS | S | M | L | XL | XXL | |
|---|---|---|---|---|---|---|---|---|
| **To fit chest measuring approximately** | | | | | | | | |
| | 16 | 18 | 20 | 22 | 24 | 26 | 28 | in |
| | 41 | 46 | 51 | 56 | 61 | 67 | 72 | cm |
| **Knitted measurements** | | | | | | | | |
| **Width across back (excluding strap)** *before felting* | | | | | | | | |
| | 18 | 19½ | 23 | 24½ | 26 | 28 | 29 | in |
| | 46 | 49.5 | 59 | 62 | 66 | 70.5 | 74 | cm |
| **Length (from center back neck)** *after felting* | | | | | | | | |
| | 8 | 8½ | 10 | 11 | 12 | 14½ | 15½ | in |
| | 20 | 22 | 25 | 28 | 30 | 37 | 40 | cm |

## Abbreviations
**Kfb** = knit into front and back of st to increase one st.
See page 9 for other abbreviations.

## Coat

Using US 8 (5 mm) needles and A, cast on 88 (94: 112: 118: 126: 134: 140) sts.

Beg with a K row, work in st st *either* foll stripe patt for striped version *or* using A only for plain version until coat measures 19½ (21½: 24½: 27½: 29½: 38: 39½) in/50 (55: 62.5: 70: 75: 92.5: 100) cm from cast-on edge, ending with a WS row.

### Shape neck

Keeping patt correct as set throughout, cont as foll:

**Next row (RS)** K39 (41: 49: 51: 53: 55: 57) sts, then turn, leaving rem sts on a holder.

Cast/bind off 3 sts at beg of next row. 36 (38: 46: 48: 50: 52: 54) sts.

Dec 1 st at neck edge of next 3 rows. 33 (35: 43: 45: 47: 49: 51) sts.

Work 1 row.

Dec 1 st at neck edge of next row and foll 2 alt rows. 30 (32: 40: 42: 44: 46: 48) sts.

Work straight/even until coat measures 36½ (39½: 43½: 47½: 51: 61: 67½) in/93 (100: 110: 121: 129: 155: 171) cm from cast-on edge, ending with a WS row.

Cast/bind off.

With RS facing, rejoin yarn to rem sts and, keeping patt correct as set throughout, cast/bind off 10 (12: 14: 16: 20: 24: 26) sts, knit to end. 39 (41: 49: 51: 53: 55: 57) sts.

**Next row (WS)** P to last 2 sts, P2tog. 38 (40: 48: 50: 52: 54: 56) sts.

Cast/bind off 2 sts at beg of next row. 36 (38: 46: 48: 50: 52: 54) sts.

Dec 1 st at neck edge of next 4 rows. 32 (34: 42: 44: 46: 48: 50) sts.

Work 1 row.

Dec 1 st at neck edge of next row and foll alt row. 30 (32: 40: 42: 44: 46: 48) sts.

Work straight/even until coat measures 36½ (39½: 43½: 47½: 51: 61: 67½) in/93 (100: 110: 121: 129: 155: 171) cm from cast-on edge, ending with a WS row.

Cast/bind off.

## Strap

Using US 8 (5 mm) needles and A, cast on 10 sts.
**Row 1 (RS)** Kfb, K8, Kfb. 12 sts.
**Row 2** P to end.
**Row 3** Kfb, K10, Kfb. 14 sts.
Beg with a P row, cont in st st until strap measures 13 (17½: 22: 27: 32: 36: 40) in/33 (44.5: 56: 68.5: 81: 91.5: 101.5) cm from cast-on edge, ending with a WS row.
**Next row (RS)** K2tog, K10, K2tog. 12 sts.
**Next row** P to end.
**Next row** K2tog, K8, K2tog. 10 sts.
Cast/bind off on WS.

## Stripe pattern

Beg with a K row and working in st st, rep foll 35 rows as necessary to form stripe patt:
4 rows A, 2 rows B, 3 rows A, 1 row C, 4 rows A, 3 rows D, 5 rows A, 3 rows C, 3 rows A, 1 row B, 4 rows A, and 2 rows D.

## To finish

Baste knitted pieces to a piece of fabric and machine-wash in hot water. Repeat if necessary, increasing water temperature each time, until knitting is felted.
Using A for striped version or B for plain version, work blanket stitch around edges of coat and strap.
Using the photograph as a guide, cut two buttonholes on one front opening edge of the coat and one buttonhole at each end of the strap. Then edge all four buttonholes with blanket stitch, using A for the striped version or B for the plain version.
Sew on buttons to correspond with buttonholes.

# Funky dawg

Here you will find designs for the trendy dog about town. The coats in this chapter use bright colors and bold textures so your dog will not only be warm and cozy but is sure to be noticed when you take him out for a walk. Why not keep your dog even warmer with a matching pair of leg warmers too?

# 1 Stripy coat and leg warmers

Why stop at just a coat? This Fair Isle striped coat has a matching set of leg warmers to keep your pooch's ankles warm. The bold shades and geometrical design are a must for any canine wardrobe.

### Yarn

1 (1: 1: 2: 2: 2: 2) 1¾ oz/50 g balls of Rowan *4 ply Soft* in main shade **A** (red/Honk 374), one ball each in **B** (salmon/Sandalwood 392), **C** (blue/Blue Bird 369), **D** (turquoise/Folly 391), **E** (green/Goblin 379), and 1 (1: 1: 1: 2: 2: 2) balls each in **F** (cream/Nippy 376), and **G** (dark grey/Sooty 372)

### Needles and extras

Pair each of US 2 (2¾ mm) and US 3 (3¼ mm) knitting needles
4 (4: 4: 4: 5: 5: 5) x ⅝ in/15 mm diameter buttons
2 press-stud fasteners/ snaps

### Tension/Gauge

28 sts and 36 rows to 4 in/10 cm over stocking/ stockinette stitch using US 3 (3¼ mm) needles

### Sizes and measurements

| | XXS | XS | S | M | L | XL | XXL | |
|---|---|---|---|---|---|---|---|---|
| **To fit chest measuring approximately** | | | | | | | | |
| | 16 | 18 | 20 | 22 | 24 | 26 | 28 | in |
| | 41 | 46 | 51 | 56 | 61 | 67 | 72 | cm |

**Knitted measurements**
**Width across back (excluding edging and strap)**

| XXS | XS | S | M | L | XL | XXL | |
|---|---|---|---|---|---|---|---|
| 12½ | 14 | 14 | 15 | 16¾ | 17½ | 18½ | in |
| 32 | 35 | 36 | 38 | 42.5 | 44.5 | 47 | cm |

**Length (from center back neck, excluding neckband)**

| XXS | XS | S | M | L | XL | XXL | |
|---|---|---|---|---|---|---|---|
| 8 | 8½ | 10 | 11 | 12 | 14½ | 15½ | in |
| 20 | 22 | 25 | 28 | 30 | 37 | 40 | cm |

### Abbreviations

See page 9 for abbreviations.

## Coat

Using US 2 (2¾ mm) needles and A, cast on 90 (96: 102: 108: 120: 126: 132) sts.

Work 4 rows in garter st (knit every row).

Change to US 3 (3¼ mm) needles.

Beg with a K row, work in st st, foll chart for patt from chart row 1, until coat measures 8 (8½: 10: 11: 12: 14½: 15½) in/20 (22: 25: 28: 30: 37: 40) cm from cast-on edge, ending with a WS row.

### Shape neck

Keeping chart patt correct throughout, cont as foll:

**Next row (RS)** Patt 34 (36: 38: 40: 44: 46: 48), then turn, leaving rem sts on a holder.

Cast/bind off 3 sts at beg of next row. 31 (33: 35: 37: 41: 43: 45) sts.

Dec 1 st at neck edge of next 4 rows. 27 (29: 31: 33: 37: 39: 41) sts.

Work 1 row.

Dec 1 st at neck edge of next row and foll alt row. 25 (27: 29: 31: 35: 37: 39) sts.

Work 3 rows.

Dec 1 st at neck edge of next row and foll 4th row. 23 (25: 27: 29: 33: 35: 37) sts.

Work straight/even until coat measures 12½ (14: 15: 16½: 18½: 22: 24½) in/32 (35: 38: 42: 47: 56: 62) cm from cast-on edge, ending with a WS row.

Change to US 2 (2¾ mm) needles.

Break off contrasting yarns and cont with A only:

Knit 1 row.

**Buttonhole row (WS)** K2, *K2tog, yf/yo, K7, rep from * to last 3 (5: 7: 9: 4: 6: 8) sts, K2tog, yf/yo, K to end. 3 (3: 3: 3: 4: 4: 4) buttonholes.

Work 2 rows more in garter st.

Cast/bind off.

With RS facing and using US 3 (3¼ mm) needles, rejoin yarn to rem sts and, keeping chart patt correct throughout, cast/bind off 22 (24: 26: 28: 32: 34: 36) sts, knit to end. 34 (36: 38: 40: 44: 46: 48) sts.

**Next row (WS)** P in patt to last 2 sts, P2tog. 33 (35: 37: 39: 43: 45: 47) sts.

Cast/bind off 2 sts at beg of next row. 31 (33: 35: 37: 41: 43: 45) sts.

Dec 1 st at neck edge of next 4 rows. 27 (29: 31: 33: 37: 39: 41) sts.

Work 1 row.

Dec 1 st at neck edge of next row and foll alt row. 25 (27: 29: 31: 35: 37: 39) sts.

Work 3 rows.

Dec 1 st at neck edge of next row and foll 4th row. 23 (25: 27: 29: 33: 35: 37) sts.

Work straight/even until coat measures 12½ (14: 15: 16½: 18½: 22: 24½) in/32 (35: 38: 42: 47: 56: 62) cm from cast-on edge, ending with a WS row.

Change to US 2 (2¾ mm) needles.

Break off contrasting yarns and cont with A only:

Work 4 rows in garter st.

Cast/bind off.

## Neckband

Press coat lightly on WS following instructions on yarn label and avoiding garter st.

With RS facing and using US 2 (2¾ mm) needles and A, pick up and knit 34 (38: 41: 45: 50: 62: 69) sts down right side of neck, 22 (24: 26: 28: 32: 34: 36) sts across back neck and 34 (38: 41: 45: 50: 62: 69) sts up left side of neck. 90 (98: 106: 118: 132: 156: 174) sts.

Knit 1 row.

**Buttonhole row** K2 , K2tog, yf/yo, K to end.

Work 2 rows more in garter st.

Cast/bind off.

## Side edgings

### Right side

With RS facing and using US 2 (2¾ mm) needles and A, pick up and knit 93 (101: 109: 121: 135: 159: 177) sts along right side of coat from cast-on edge to cast-/bound-off edge.

Work 4 rows in garter st.

Cast/bind off.

### Left side

With RS facing and using US 2 (2¾ mm) needles and A, pick up and knit 93 (101: 109: 121: 135: 159: 177) sts along left side of coat from cast-/bound-off edge to cast-on edge.

Work 4 rows in garter st.

Cast/bind off.

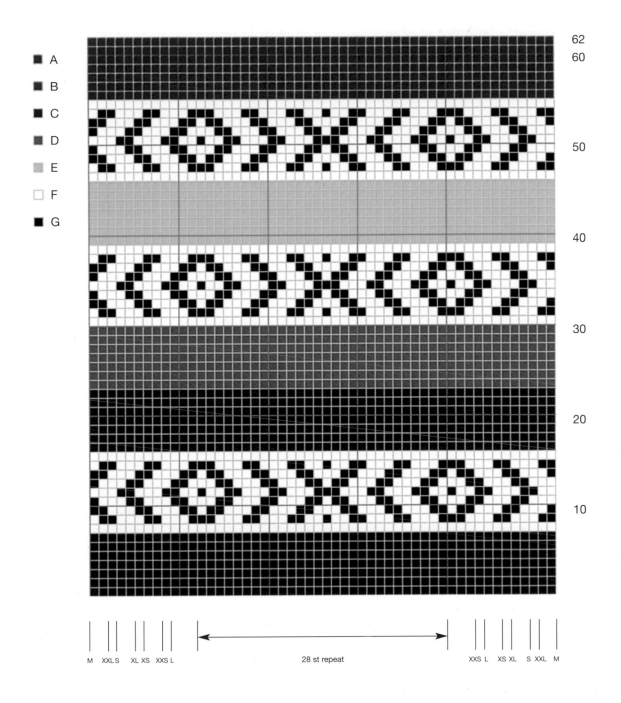

A
B
C
D
E
F
G

62
60

50

40

30

20

10

M   XXL S   XL XS   XXS L          28 st repeat          XXS L   XS XL   S XXL   M

## Strap

Using US 2 (2¾ mm) needles and A, cast on 11 (11: 11: 13: 15: 17: 17) sts.

**Row 1** *K1, P1, rep from * to last st, K1.

Last row is repeated to form moss/seed st patt.

Cont in moss/seed st until strap measures 9 (10: 11¼: 12½: 13½: 14½: 15½) in/23.5 (26: 28.5: 32: 34: 37: 40) cm from cast-on edge.

Cast/bind off in moss/seed st.

## To finish

Sew cast-on edge of the strap to inside of coat so that it will sit just behind the foreleg. Sew press-stud fasteners/snaps to cast-/bound-off edge of strap and to inside of coat to correspond.

Sew on buttons to correspond with buttonholes.

## Leg warmers (make 2)

Using US 2 (2¾ mm) needles and A, cast on 46 (46: 50: 50: 58: 58: 58) sts.

**Rib row 1** K2, *P2, K2, rep from * to end.

**Rib row 2** P2, *K2, P2, rep from * to end.

Last 2 rows are repeated to form rib patt.

Work 6 rows more in rib.

Change to US 3 (3¼ mm) needles.

Work 6 rows more in rib.

Breaking off and joining in yarns as required and cont in rib throughout, work stripes as foll:

**Work 12 rows B, 12 rows C, 12 rows D and 12 rows E.**

**Sizes L, XL and XXL only:**

Rep from ** to ** once more.

**All sizes:**

Cont with A only, work 6 rows in rib.

Change to US 2 (2¾ mm) needles.

Work 6 rows more in rib.

Cast/bind off in rib.

## To finish

Sew side seams.

# 2 Denim-style jacket

What could be more fashionable for a walk in the local park than this rugged, denim-style jacket? Your dog will love to strut his stuff in this coat, which is complete with pocket flaps and buttons.

## Yarn
3 (3: 4: 5: 6: 7: 8) 1¾ oz/50 g balls of Rowan *Denim* in mid-blue/Memphis 229

## Needles and extras
Pair each of US 3 (3¼ mm) and US 6 (4 mm) knitting needles
5 (5: 5: 7: 7: 7: 7) x ⅜ in/10 mm diameter buttons
7 (7: 8: 8: 9: 9: 10) press-stud fasteners/snaps

## Tension/Gauge
20 sts and 28 rows to 4 in/10 cm *before washing* over stocking/stockinette stitch using US 6 (4 mm) needles.

## Note:
Rowan Denim is a unique yarn which shrinks and fades like denim fabric on the initial wash. This pattern has been written with this shrinkage taken into account. For this reason, yarn substitution is inadvisable.

## Sizes and measurements

| XXS | XS | S | M | L | XL | XXL | |
|-----|-----|-----|-----|-----|-----|-----|-----|

**To fit chest measuring approximately**

| XXS | XS | S | M | L | XL | XXL | |
|-----|-----|-----|-----|-----|-----|-----|-----|
| 16 | 18 | 20 | 22 | 24 | 26 | 28 | in |
| 41 | 46 | 51 | 56 | 60 | 67 | 72 | cm |

**Knitted measurements**
**To fit chest measuring approximately**

| XXS | XS | S | M | L | XL | XXL | |
|-----|-----|-----|-----|-----|-----|-----|-----|
| 17¾ | 20¾ | 22 | 24½ | 26½ | 28½ | 30¾ | in |
| 45 | 52 | 56 | 62 | 67 | 72 | 78 | cm |

**Length (after washing) (from center back neck edge, excluding collar)**

| XXS | XS | S | M | L | XL | XXL | |
|-----|-----|-----|-----|-----|-----|-----|-----|
| 10½ | 11½ | 13½ | 15¾ | 17¾ | 20 | 22 | in |
| 27 | 29 | 34 | 40 | 45 | 51 | 56 | cm |

## Abbreviations
See page 9 for abbreviations.

## Jacket

With US 3 (3¼ mm) needles, cast on 90 (104: 112: 124: 134: 144: 156) sts.

**Row 1 (RS)** *K1, P1, rep from * to end.

**Row 2 (WS)** *P1, K1, rep * to end.

Last 2 rows are repeated to form moss/seed st patt.

Work 6 rows more in moss/seed st.

Change to US 6 (4 mm) needles.

**Patt row 1 (RS)** K42 (49: 53: 59: 63: 69: 75), [P1, K1] 3 times, K to last st, pick up loop between needles and place on right needle, sl 1. (Loop picked up does not count as a stitch.)

**Patt row 2** P tog first st and loop, P41 (48: 52: 58: 62: 68: 74), [K1, P1] 3 times, P to last st, pick up loop between needles and place on right needle, sl 1.

**Patt row 3** K tog first st and loop tbl, K41 (48: 52: 58: 62: 68: 74), [P1, K1] 3 times, K to last st, pick up loop between needles and place on right needle, sl 1.

Last 2 rows (patt rows 2 and 3) are repeated to form patt (st st with central 6-st moss/seed st band and slip st edging).

Cont in patt until jacket measures 6½ (7¾: 10¼: 12½: 15: 17¾: 20) in/17 (20: 26: 32: 38: 45: 51) cm from cast-on edge, ending with a WS row (patt row 2).

### Divide for leg holes

### Left side

**Next row (RS)** Patt 34 (39: 42: 46: 52: 55: 60), K2tog, then turn, leaving rem sts on a holder.

Working on these 35 (40: 43: 47: 53: 56: 61) sts only and keeping slip st edging correct throughout, cont as foll:

**Next row** P to last st, pick up loop between needles and place on right needle, sl 1.

**Next row** K tog first st and loop tbl, K to last 2 sts, K2tog. 34 (39: 42: 46: 52: 55: 60) sts.

Rep last 2 rows 9 times more. 25 (30: 33: 37: 42: 46: 51) sts.

**Next row** P to last st, pick up loop between needles and place on right needle, sl 1.

Place these sts on another holder and DO NOT break off yarn but set this ball aside to use later.

### Chest section

With RS facing, rejoin yarn to rem sts on first holder and cast/bind off 1 (1: 1: 2: 2: 2: 2) sts, K2tog tbl, lift 2nd st on right needle over first st and off needle, K2 (4: 5: 6: 6: 7: 8),

[K1, P1] 3 times, K2 (4: 5: 6: 6: 7: 8), K2tog, turn, leaving rem sts on holder.

Working on these 12 (16: 18: 20: 20: 22: 24) sts only, cont as foll:

**Next row (WS)** P3 (5: 6: 7: 7: 8: 9), [P1, K1] 3 times, P3 (5: 6: 7: 7: 8: 9).

**Next row** K3 (5: 6: 7: 7: 8: 9), [K1, P1] 3 times, K3 (5: 6: 7: 7: 8: 9).

Rep last 2 rows 9 times more.

**Next row** P3 (5: 6: 6: 7: 8: 9), [P1, K1] 3 times, P3 (5: 6: 6: 7: 8: 9).

Break off yarn and place these sts on a 2nd holder.

### Right side

With RS facing, rejoin yarn to rem sts and cast/bind off 1 (1: 1: 2: 2: 2: 2) sts, K2tog tbl, lift 2nd st on right needle over first st and off needle, K to last st, pick up loop between needles and place on right needle, sl 1.

Working on these 35 (40: 43: 47: 52: 56: 61) sts only and keeping slip st edging correct, cont as foll:

**Next row** P tog first st and loop, P to end.

**Next row** K2tog tbl, K to last st, pick up loop between needles and place on right needle, sl 1. 34 (39: 42: 46: 51: 55: 60) sts.

Rep last 2 rows 9 times more. 25 (30: 33: 37: 42: 46: 51) sts.

**Next row** P tog first st and loop, P to end.

Break off yarn and place these sts on a 3rd holder.

### Leghole edgings (both alike)

With RS facing and using US 3 (3¼ mm) needles, cast on 1 st, pick up and knit 13 sts down side of leg hole, 4 (4: 4: 6: 6: 6: 6) sts across base of hole and 13 sts up second side. 31 (31: 31: 33: 33: 33: 33) sts.

**Row 1** Cast on 1 st, *K1, P1, rep from * to last st, K1. 32 (32: 32: 34: 34: 34: 34) sts.

**Row 2** *K1, P1, rep from * to end.

**Row 3** *P1, K1, rep from * to end.

Cast/bind off in moss/seed st.

### Join sections

With RS facing and using ball yarn previously set aside, K tog first st and loop tbl, K22 (27: 30: 34: 39: 43: 48), K2tog, from 1st holder, K3 (5: 6: 7: 7: 8: 9), [K1, P1] 3 times, K3 (5: 6: 7: 7: 8: 9), from 2nd holder, K2tog tbl, K22 (27: 30: 34: 39: 43: 48), pick up loop between needles and place on right needle, sl 1 from 3rd holder. 60 (74: 82: 92: 102: 112: 124) sts.

**Next row (WS)** P tog first st and loop, P26 (33: 37: 42: 47: 52: 58), [K1, P1] 3 times, P to last st, pick up loop between needles and place on right needle, sl 1.

**Next row** K tog first st and loop through the back of loops, K26 (33: 37: 41: 47: 52: 58), [P1, K1] 3 times, K to last st, pick up loop between needles and place on right needle, sl 1.

Last 2 rows are repeated to form patt (st st with central 6-st moss/seed st band and slip-st edging).

Work 17 rows more in patt as set.

Cast/bind off in patt.

## Right collar

With US 3 (3¼ mm) needles, cast on 43 (49: 53: 57: 63: 69: 75) sts.

**Row 1 (RS)** *K1, P1, rep from * to last st, K1.

Last row is repeated to form moss/seed st patt.

Work 3 rows more in moss/seed st.

**Next row** K1; P1, K1, P3tog, work in moss/seed st to end. 41 (47: 51: 55: 61: 67: 73) sts.

Work 3 rows in moss/seed st.

Rep last 4 rows 5 times more. 31 (37: 41: 45: 51: 57: 63) sts.

Cast/bind off in moss/seed st.

## Left collar

With US 3 (3¼ mm) needles, cast on 43 (49: 53: 57: 63: 69: 75) sts.

Work 4 rows in moss/seed st as for right collar.

**Next row** Work in moss/seed st to last 6 sts, P3tog, K1, P1, K1. 41 (47: 51: 55: 61: 67: 73) sts.

Work 3 rows in moss/seed st.

Rep last 4 rows 5 times more. 31 (37: 41: 45: 51: 57: 63) sts.

Cast/bind off in moss/seed st.

## Pocket flaps (make 2)

With US 3 (3¼ mm) needles, cast on 19 (19: 23: 23: 27: 27: 31) sts.

Work 3 rows in moss/seed st as for right collar.

**Next row** Work 4 sts in moss/seed st, P3tog, work in moss/seed st to last 7 sts, P3tog, work 4 sts in moss/seed st.

**Next row** *K1, P1, rep from * to last st, K1.

Rep last 2 rows until 11 sts rem.

**Next row** [K1, P1] twice, sl 1, K2tog, psso, [P1, K1] twice. 9 sts.

**Next row** K1, P1, K1, sl 1, K2tog, psso, K1, P1, K1. 7 sts.

**Next row** K1, P1, sl 1, K2tog, psso, P1, K1. 5 sts.

**Next row** K1, sl 1, K2tog, psso, K1. 3 sts.

**Next row** Sl 1, K2tog, psso.

Fasten off.

## To finish

Machine-wash all pieces at 140ºF/60ºC and allow to dry completely.

Press coat lightly on WS, following instructions on yarn label and avoiding moss/seed st.

Sew leghole edging seams and sew cast-on stitches to jacket. Sew collar section to neck edge, matching straight edge to center back opening edges. Using the photograph as a guide, sew pocket flaps to back of jacket. Sew one button to each point of pocket flaps. Sew remaining buttons equally spaced along central moss/seed stitch band, starting at the neck edge. Sew press-stud fasteners/snaps along centre back opening, one at neck edge, one at the cast on edge and the others evenly spaced between.

# 3 Herringbone bones

This chic coat is really easy to knit, with the bone motifs embroidered on to the finished coat. Add the bones wherever you like – to the bottom corners, as here, or all over for a really stunning effect.

### Yarn
2 (2: 3: 3: 3: 4: 4) 1¾ oz/50 g balls of Rowan *4 ply Soft* in main shade **A** (black/Black 383) and one ball in **B** (cream/Nippy 376)

### Needles and extras
Pair each of US 2 (2¾ mm) and US 3 (3¼ mm) knitting needles
4 (4: 4: 4: 5: 5: 5) x ⅝ in/15 mm (bone-shaped) buttons
2 press-stud fasteners/snaps

### Tension/Gauge
28 sts and 36 rows to 4 in/10 cm over stocking/stockinette stitch using US 3 (3¼ mm) needles

### Abbreviations
See page 9 for abbreviations.

### Sizes and measurements

| | XXS | XS | S | M | L | XL | XXL | |
|---|---|---|---|---|---|---|---|---|
| **To fit chest measuring approximately** | | | | | | | | |
| | 16 | 18 | 20 | 22 | 24 | 26 | 28 | in |
| | 41 | 46 | 51 | 56 | 61 | 67 | 72 | cm |
| **Knitted measurements** | | | | | | | | |
| **Width across back (excluding strap)** | | | | | | | | |
| | 12½ | 14 | 14 | 15 | 16¾ | 17½ | 18½ | in |
| | 32 | 34 | 36 | 38 | 42.5 | 46.5 | 50 | cm |
| **Length (from center back neck edge, excluding neckband)** | | | | | | | | |
| | 8 | 8½ | 10 | 11 | 12 | 14½ | 15½ | in |
| | 20 | 22 | 25 | 28 | 30 | 37 | 40 | cm |

## Coat

Using US 2 (2¾ mm) needles and A, cast on 90 (96: 102: 108: 120: 126: 132) sts.

**Row 1 (WS)** *K1, P1, rep from * to end.

**Row 2** *P1, K1, rep from * to end.

Last 2 rows are repeated to form moss/seed st patt.

Work 3 rows more in moss/seed st, ending with a row 1.

Change to 3¾ mm (US 3) needles and continue as foll:

**Patt row 1 (RS)** [P1, K1] twice, P1, K to last 4 sts, [P1, K1] twice.

**Patt row 2** [K1, P1] twice, K1, P to last 4 sts, [K1, P1] twice.

Last 2 rows are repeated to form patt (st st with 5-st moss/seed st borders).

Cont in patt until coat measures 8 (8½: 10: 11: 11½: 14½:

B   Swiss darn/duplicate stitch

15½) in/20 (22: 25: 28: 30: 37: 40) cm from cast-on edge, ending with a WS row.

**Shape neck**

Keeping patt correct throughout, cont as foll:

**Next row (RS)** Patt 34 (36: 38: 40: 44: 46: 48), then turn, leaving rem sts on a holder.

Cast/bind off 3 sts at beg of next row. 31 (33: 35: 37: 41: 43: 45) sts.

Dec 1 st at neck edge of next 4 rows. 27 (29: 31: 33: 37: 39: 41) sts.

Work 1 row.

Dec 1 st at neck edge of next row and foll alt row. 25 (27: 29: 31: 35: 37: 39) sts.

Work 3 rows.

Dec 1 st at neck edge of next row and foll 4th row. 23 (25: 27: 29: 33: 35: 37) sts.

Work straight/even until coat measures 12½ (14: 15: 16: 18½: 22: 24½) in/32 (35: 38: 42: 47: 56: 62) cm from cast-on edge, ending with a WS row.

Change to US 2 (2¾ mm) needles.

**Next row (RS)** * K1, P1, rep from * to last st, K1.

Last row is repeated to form moss/seed st patt.

**Buttonhole row** Moss/seed st 2, * K2tog, yf/yo, moss/seed st 7, rep from * to last 3 (5: 7: 9: 4: 6: 8) sts, K2tog, moss/seed st to end. 3 (3: 3: 3: 4: 4: 4) buttonholes.

Work 2 rows more in moss/seed stitch.

Cast/bind off.

With RS facing, rejoin A to rem sts and, keeping patt correct throughout, cast/bind off 22 (24: 26: 28: 32: 34: 36) sts, patt to end. 34 (36: 38: 40: 44: 46: 48) sts.

**Next row (WS)** Patt to last 2 sts, P2tog. 33 (35: 37: 39: 43: 45: 47) sts.

Cast/bind off 2 sts at beg of next row. 31 (33: 35: 37: 41: 43: 45) sts.

Dec 1 st at neck edge of next 4 rows. 27 (29: 31: 33: 37: 39: 41) sts.

Work 1 row.

Dec 1 st at neck edge of next row and foll alt row. 25 (27: 29: 31: 35: 37: 39) sts.

Work 3 rows.

Dec 1 st at neck edge of next row and foll 4th row. 23 (25: 27: 29: 33: 35: 37) sts.

Work straight/even until coat measures 12½ (14: 15: 16: 18½: 22: 24½) in/32 (35: 38: 42: 47: 56: 62) cm from cast-on edge, ending with a WS row.

Change to US 2 (2¾ mm) needles.

**Next row (RS)** * K1, P1, rep from * to last st, K1.

Last row is repeated to form moss/seed st patt.

Work 3 rows more in moss/seed st.

Cast/bind off.

## Neckband

Press coat lightly on WS, following instructions on yarn label and avoiding moss/seed st.

With RS facing and using US 2 (2¾ mm) needles and A, pick up and knit 34 (38: 41: 45: 50: 62: 69) sts down right side of neck, 22 (24: 26: 28: 32: 34: 36) sts across back neck, and 34 (38: 41: 45: 50: 62: 69) sts up left side of neck. 90 (98: 106: 118: 132: 156: 174) sts.

**Next row** * K1, P1, rep from * to end.

**Buttonhole row** P1, K1, P2tog, yf/yo, moss/seed st to end.

Work 2 rows more in moss/seed st.

Cast/bind off.

## Strap

Using US 2 (2¾ mm) needles and A, cast on 17 (19: 21: 23: 25: 27: 27) sts.

**Row 1** *K1, P1, rep from * to last st, K1.

Last row is repeated to form moss/seed st patt.

Cont in moss/seed st until strap measures 9 (10: 11¼: 12½: 13½: 14½: 15½) in/23.5 (26: 28.5: 32: 34: 37: 40) cm from cast-on edge.

Cast/bind off in moss/seed st.

## To finish

Using B and a blunt-ended yarn needle, Swiss darn/duplicate st desired number of bones on coat, following chart for bone motif.

Using B, embroider a line of running stitches on the middle stitch of the moss/seed stitch edging of the coat. Sew cast-on edge of strap to inside of coat so that it will sit just behind the foreleg. Sew press-stud fasteners/snaps to cast-/bound-off edge of strap and to inside of coat to correspond.

Sew on buttons to correspond with buttonholes.

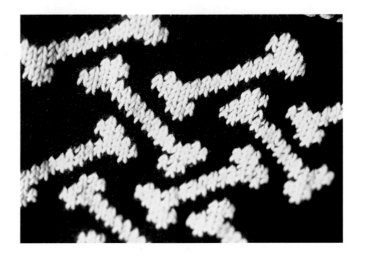

# 4 Deep-rib zip-up

This deep-rib collared sweater makes an ideal winter garment for the larger dog. Easy to zip up, it is great for impromptu outings, and the sweater design, complete with legs, ensures your dog is toasty warm.

### Yarn
4 (4: 5: 5) 3½ oz/100 g balls of Rowan *Plaid* in turquoise/Creeper 155

### Needles and extras
Pair each of US 10½ (7 mm) and US 11 (8 mm) knitting needles
Zipper to fit
Thin round elastic (optional)

### Tension/Gauge
11 sts and 14 rows to 4 in/10 cm over stocking/stockinette stitch using US 11 (8 mm) needles.

### Abbreviations
See page 9 for abbreviations.

### Sizes and measurements

| M | L | XL | XXL | |
|---|---|----|-----|---|

**To fit chest measuring approximately**

| M | L | XL | XXL | |
|------|----|------|------|-----|
| 22 | 24 | 26 | 28 | in |
| 56 | 61 | 67 | 72 | cm |

**Knitted measurements**
**Around chest**

| M | L | XL | XXL | |
|------|----|------|-----|-----|
| 30½ | 32 | 33½ | 35 | in |
| 76.5 | 81 | 84.5 | 89 | cm |

**Length (from center back neck edge, excluding collar)**

| M | L | XL | XXL | |
|----|------|------|------|-----|
| 20 | 21½ | 23 | 25 | in |
| 51 | 55 | 59.5 | 64.5 | cm |

## Sweater

Using US 10½ (7 mm) needles, cast on 75 (79: 83: 87) sts.

**Rib row 1 (RS)** K3, *P1, K3, rep from * to end.

**Rib row 2** K1, P2, *K1, P3, rep from * to last 3 sts, P2, K1.

Last 2 rows are repeated to form rib patt.

Cont in rib until sweater measures 5½ (6½: 7: 7¾) in/14 (16: 18: 20) cm from cast-on edge, ending with a RS row.

**Inc row (WS)** K1, P2, *inc in next st, P3, K1, P3, rep from * to last 8 (4: 8: 4) sts, inc in next st, P3 (0: 3: 0), K1, P2, K1. 84 (89: 93: 98) sts.

Change to US 11 (8 mm) needles.

**Patt row 1 (RS)** K to end.

**Patt row 2** K1, P to last st, K1.

Last 2 rows are repeated to form patt (st st with 1-st garter st borders).

Cont in patt until sweater measures 11 (12½: 14: 15½) in/ 28 (32: 35: 40) cm from cast-on edge, ending with a WS row.

### Divide for leg holes

Keeping patt correct throughout, cont as foll:

**Next row (RS)** Patt 34 (36: 38: 40), K2tog, then turn, leaving rem sts on a holder.

Working on these 35 (37: 38: 41) sts only, cont as foll:

Work 1 row.

Dec 1 st at leg hole edge of next row and foll 8 alt rows. 26 (28: 30: 32) sts.

Work 1 row.

Place these sts on another holder and DO NOT break off yarn but set this ball aside to use later.

With RS facing, join a new ball of yarn at first leg divide on first holder and K12 (13: 13: 14), then turn, leaving rem sts on holder.

Working on these 13 (13: 14: 14) sts only and beg with a P row, work 19 rows in st st.

Break off yarn and place these sts on a 3rd holder.

With RS facing, rejoin yarn to rem 36 (38: 40: 42) sts on first holder and, keeping patt correct throughout, K2tog tbl, knit to end. 35 (37: 39: 41) sts.

Work 1 row.

Dec 1 st at leg hole edge of next row and foll 8 alt rows. 26 (28: 30: 32) sts.

Work 1 row.

## Join sections

Slide all 64 (69: 73: 78) sts on to one needle and with RS facing and using ball of yarn set aside previously, cont as foll:

**Next row (RS)** K25 (27: 29: 31), K2tog, K1, K2tog tbl, K4 (5: 5: 6), K2tog, K1, K2tog tbl, K to end. 60 (65: 69: 74) sts.

Work 1 row.

**Next row** K24 (26: 28: 30), K2tog, K1, K2tog tbl, K3 (4: 4: 5), K2tog, K1, K2tog tbl, K to end. 56 (61: 65: 70) sts.

Work 1 row.

**Next row** K23 (25: 27: 29), K2tog, K1, K2tog tbl, K2 (3: 3: 4), K2tog, K1, K2tog tbl K to end. 52 (57: 61: 66) sts.

Work 1 row.

**Next row** K22 (24: 26: 28), K2tog, K4 (5: 5: 6), K2tog, K to end. 50 (55: 59: 64) sts.

Work 1 row.

**Next row** K21 (23: 25: 27), K2tog, K4 (5: 5: 6), K2tog, K to end. 48 (53: 57: 62) sts.

Work 1 row.

**Size M only:**

**Next row** K23, K2tog, K to end. 47 sts.

**Sizes L, XL and XXL only:**

**Next row** K (22: 24: 26), K2tog, K (5: 5: 6), K2tog, K to end. (51: 55: 60) sts.

**All sizes:**
Work 1 row.
**Size XL only:**
Work 2 rows straight/even.
**Size XXL only:**
**Next row** K29, K2tog, K to end. 59 sts.
Work 1 row.

## Collar

**All sizes:**
Change to US 10½ (7 mm) needles.
**Next row (RS)** K3, *P1, K3, rep from * to end.
**Next row** K2tog, P1, *K1, P3, rep from * to last 4 sts, K1, P1, K2tog.
**Next row** Inc in first st, K1, *P1, K3, rep from * to last 3 sts, P1, K1, inc in last st.
Set rib patt on next 2 rows as foll:
**Rib row 1** K1, P2, *K1, P3, rep from * to last 4 sts, K1, P2, K1.
**Rib row 2** K3, *P1, K3, rep from * to end.
Last 2 rows are repeated to form rib patt.
Cont in rib until collar measures 3 in/8 cm from start of ribbing.
Change to US 11 (8 mm) needles.

Cont in rib until collar measures 4¼ (4¼: 5: 6½) in/11 (11: 13: 16) cm from start of ribbing, ending with a rib row 2.
Cast/bind off loosely in rib.

## Sleeves (both alike)

Using US 10½ (7 mm) needles, cast on 35 sts.
**Rib row 1** K3, *P1, K3, rep from * to end.
**Rib row 2** P3, *K1, P3, rep from * to end.
Rep last 2 rows until sleeve measures 8 in/20 cm from cast-on edge, ending with a rib row 2.
Cast/bind off loosely in rib.

## To finish

Do not press.
Sew together row ends of sleeves.
Set cast-/bound-off edge of sleeves into leg holes, positioning sleeve seams at beginning of leg divisions.
Sew zipper into opening, reversing sides at notch at beginning of collar.
If necessary for fit, thread lengths of elastic through the WS of the lower ribbed section, securing firmly at the zipper edges.

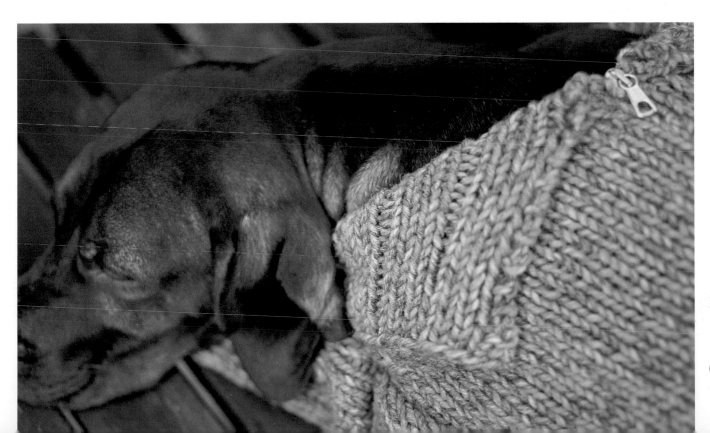

# 5 Warm and woolly

This simple coat knits quickly in a chunky yarn so your dog will have a comfy coat in no time. The addition of bold buttons along the back finishes the garment and also makes dressing your dog trouble-free.

## Yarn
2 (2: 3: 3: 4: 4: 5) 3½ oz/100 g balls of Rowan *Chunky Print* in blue/Deep End 076 *or* multicoloured/Swizzle 075

## Needles and extras
Pair each of US 10½ (7 mm) and US 11 (8 mm) knitting needles
10 (10: 10: 10: 12: 12: 12) x 1 in/25 mm diameter buttons

## Tension/Gauge
11 sts and 14 rows to 4 in/10 cm over stocking/stockinette stitch using US 11 (8 mm) needles.

## Abbreviations
See page 9 for abbreviations.

## Sizes and measurements

| | XXS | XS | S | M | L | XL | XXL | |
|---|---|---|---|---|---|---|---|---|
| **To fit chest measuring approximately** | | | | | | | | |
| | 16 | 18 | 20 | 22 | 24 | 26 | 28 | in |
| | 41 | 46 | 51 | 56 | 61 | 67 | 72 | cm |
| **Knitted measurements** | | | | | | | | |
| **Around chest** | | | | | | | | |
| | 19½ | 22 | 24 | 26 | 28 | 30½ | 32½ | in |
| | 50 | 55.5 | 61 | 66 | 72 | 77 | 83 | cm |
| **Length (from center back neck edge)** | | | | | | | | |
| | 11½ | 12½ | 15½ | 17½ | 20 | 23 | 25½ | in |
| | 29 | 32 | 39 | 44 | 50.5 | 58.5 | 65 | cm |

## Coat

Using US 10½ (7 mm) needles, cast on 55 (61: 67: 73: 79: 85: 91) sts.

**Rib row (RS)** 1 K5, *P3, K3, rep from * to last 2 sts, K2.

**Rib row 2** K2, *P3, K3, rep from * to last 5 sts, P3, K2.

Last 2 rows are repeated to form rib patt.

Cont in rib until coat measures 2½ (2½: 2½: 3¼: 3: 3: 4) in/ 6 (6: 6: 8: 8: 8: 10) cm from cast-on edge, ending with a WS row.

Change to US 11 (8 mm) needles.

**Patt row 1 (RS)** K to end.

**Patt row 2** K2, P to last 2 sts, K2.

Last 2 rows are repeated to form patt (st st with 2-st garter st borders).

Cont in patt until coat measures 6 (7: 10: 12: 14: 17: 19) in/15 (18: 25: 30: 35: 43: 48) cm from cast-on edge, ending with a WS row.

## Divide for leg holes

**Next row (RS)** K22 (23: 24: 26: 28: 31: 34), K2tog, then turn, leaving rem sts on a holder.

Working on these 23 (24: 25: 27: 29: 32: 35) sts only, cont as foll:

**Next row** P to last 2 sts, K2.

**Next row K** to last 2 sts, K2tog. 22 (23: 24: 26: 28: 31: 34) sts.

Rep last 2 rows 3 (3: 3: 3: 4: 4: 4) times more. 19 (20: 21: 23: 24: 27: 30) sts.

**Next row** P to last 2 sts, K2.

Place these sts on another holder and DO NOT break off yarn but set this ball aside to use later.

With RS facing, rejoin yarn to rem sts and K7 (11: 15: 17: 19: 19: 19), then turn, leaving rem sts on a holder.

Working on these 7 (11: 15: 17: 19: 19: 19) sts only, work 9 (9: 9: 9: 11: 11: 11) rows in st st.

Break off yarn and leave these sts on a holder.

With RS facing, rejoin yarn to rem 24 (25: 26: 28: 30: 33: 36) sts and cont as foll:

**Next row (RS)** K2tog tbl, K to end. 23 (24: 25: 27: 29: 32: 35) sts.

**Next row** K2, P to end.

Rep last 2 rows 4 (4: 4: 4: 5: 5: 5) times more. 19 (20: 21: 23: 24: 27: 30) sts.

Break off yarn and place these sts on a holder.

### Join sections

Slide all sts on to one needle and, with RS facing and using ball of yarn previously set aside, cont as foll:

**Next row (RS)** K17 (18: 19: 21: 24: 27: 28), K2tog, 1 (1: 1: 1: 0: 0: 1) time, K7 (11: 15: 17: 19: 19: 19) (from centre gusset), K2tog tbl 1 (1: 1: 1: 0: 0: 1) time, K to end. 43 (49: 55: 61: 67: 73: 77) sts.

**Next row** K2, P to last 2 sts, K2.

**Next row** K16 (17: 18: 20: 22: 25: 27), K2tog, K7 (11: 15: 17: 19: 19: 19), K2tog tbl, K to end. 41 (47: 53: 59: 65: 71: 75) sts.

**Next row** K2, P17 (20: 23: 26: 29: 32: 34), P3tog, P to last 2 sts, K2. 39 (45: 51: 57: 63: 69: 73) sts.

### Size XXL only:

**Next row (RS)** K33, K3tog, K1, K3tog tbl, K to end. 69 sts.

**Next row** K2, P to last 2 sts, K2.

### All sizes:

Change to US 10½ (7 mm) needles.

**Next row (RS)** *K3,P3, rep from * to last 3 sts, K3.

**Next row** K2, P1, *K3, P3, rep from * to last 6 sts, K3, P1, K2.

Rep last 2 rows twice more.

Cast/bind off loosely in rib.

## To finish

Press coat lightly on WS, following instructions on yarn label and avoiding ribbing.

Using the photograph as a guide, sew on buttons in pairs (one button on right side and one button on wrong side) along one opening edge of coat. To fasten coat, push button sewn on wrong side through to right side of other edge of coat.

# 6 Double-strap jacket

With its attractive yet practical strap fastenings, this colorful coat is ideal for all your dog's favorite games. Whether he's playing frisbee, fetch or football, Fido is sure to look fabulous.

### Yarn
4 (4: 5: 5: 6: 7: 7) 1¾ oz/50 g balls of Rowan *Handknit Cotton* in main shade **A** (blue/Diana 287) and one ball each in **B** (pink/Slick 313), **C** (orange/Mango Fool 319), **D** (red/Rosso 215) and **E** (yellow/Buttercup 320)

### Needles and extras
Pair each of US 6 (4 mm) and US 7 (4½ mm) knitting needles
8 D-rings, 1 in/25 mm wide (at the straight edge)

### Tension/Gauge
19 sts and 28 rows to 4 in/10 cm over stocking/stockinette stitch using US 7 (4½ mm) needles.

### Abbreviations
See page 9 for abbreviations.

### Sizes and measurements

| | XXS | XS | S | M | L | XL | XXL | |
|---|---|---|---|---|---|---|---|---|
| **To fit chest measuring approximately** | | | | | | | | |
| | 16 | 18 | 20 | 22 | 24 | 26 | 28 | in |
| | 41 | 46 | 51 | 56 | 61 | 67 | 72 | cm |

**Knitted measurements**
**Width across back (excluding strap)**

| 12½ | 13½ | 14 | 15½ | 16 | 17½ | 20½ | in |
|---|---|---|---|---|---|---|---|
| 31.5 | 33.5 | 36 | 39 | 41 | 44 | 51.5 | cm |

**Length (from center back neck edge, excluding neckband)**

| 8 | 8½ | 10½ | 12½ | 14 | 15½ | 17 | in |
|---|---|---|---|---|---|---|---|
| 20 | 22 | 27 | 32 | 36 | 40 | 43 | cm |

## Jacket

Using US 6 (4 mm) needles and A, cast on 60 (64: 68: 74: 78: 84: 98) sts.

Work 3 rows in garter st (knit every row).

Change to US 7 (4½ mm) needles.

**Patt row 1 (WS)** K3, P to last 3 sts, K3.

**Patt row 2** K to end.

Last 2 rows are repeated to form patt (st st with 3-st garter st borders).

Cont in patt until jacket measures 8 (8½: 10½: 12½: 14: 15½: 17) in/20 (22: 27: 32: 36: 40: 43) cm from cast-on edge, ending with a WS row.

**Shape neck**

Keeping patt correct throughout, cont as foll:

**Next row (RS)** Patt 26 (28: 30: 33: 35: 37: 44), then turn, leaving rem sts on a holder.

Cast/bind off 3 sts at beg of next row. 23 (25: 27: 30: 32: 34: 41) sts.

Dec 1 st at neck edge of next 5 rows. 18 (20: 22: 25: 27: 29: 36) sts.

Work 1 row.

Dec 1 st at neck edge of next row and foll alt row. 16 (18: 20: 23: 25: 27: 34) sts.

Work straight/even until jacket measures 13½ (14½: 16½: 19: 23½: 25) in/34 (37: 42: 48: 53: 60: 64) cm from cast-on edge, ending with WS row.

Change to US 6 (4 mm) needles.

Work 3 rows in garter st.

Cast/bind off on WS.

With RS facing and using US 7 (4½ mm) needles, rejoin A to rem sts and, keeping patt correct throughout, cast/bind off 8 (8: 8: 8: 8: 10: 10) sts, patt to end. 26 (28: 30: 33: 35: 37: 44) sts.

**Next row (WS)** Patt to last 2 sts, P2tog. 25 (27: 29: 32: 34: 36: 43) sts.

Cast/bind off 2 sts at beg of next row. 23 (25: 27: 30: 32: 34: 41) sts.

Dec 1 st at neck edge of next 5 rows. 18 (20: 22: 25: 27: 29: 36) sts.

Work 1 row.

Dec 1 st at neck edge of next row and foll alt row. 16 (18: 20: 23: 25: 27: 34) sts.

Work straight/even until jacket measures 13½ (14½: 16½: 19: 21: 23½: 25) in/34 (37: 42: 48: 53: 60: 64) cm from cast-

on edge, ending with a WS row.

Change to US 6 (4 mm) needles.

Work 3 rows in garter st.

Cast/bind off on WS.

## Neckband

Press coat lightly on WS following instructions on yarn label and avoiding garter st.

With RS facing and using US 6 (4 mm) needles and A, pick up and knit 32 (34: 34: 36: 38: 43: 35) sts down right side of neck, 8 (8: 8: 8: 8: 10: 10) sts across back neck, and 32 (34: 34: 36: 38: 43: 35) sts up left side of neck. 72 (76: 76: 80: 84: 96: 100) sts.

Work 2 rows in garter st.

Cast/bind off on WS.

## Main belts (make 2)

Using US 6 (4 mm) needles and B, cast on 6 sts.

**Row 1 (RS)** K to end.

**Row 2** K1, P4, K1.

Last 2 rows are repeated to form patt.

Cont in patt until belt measures 20 (22: 24: 26: 28: 30: 32) in/51 (56: 61: 66: 71: 77: 82) cm from cast-on edge, ending with a WS row.

**Next row** K1, K2 tog, K2tog tbl, K1. 4 sts.

**Next row** K1, P2, K1.

**Next row** K2tog, K2tog tbl. 2 sts.

**Next row** K2tog.
Fasten off.
Make second belt in same way, but using C.

### Front straps (make 2)
\*\*Using US 6 (4 mm) needles and D, cast on 1 st.
**Row 1 (RS)** Inc. 2 sts.
**Row 2** Inc twice. 4 sts.
**Row 3** K1, M1, K2, M1, K1. 6 sts.
**Row 4 (WS)** K1, P4, K1.
**Row 5 (RS)** K to end.
Last 2 rows are repeated to form patt.\*\*
Cont in patt until strap measures 8 in/20 cm from cast-on edge, ending with a WS row.
**Next row** K1, K2 tog, K2tog tbl, K1. 4 sts.
**Next row** K1, P2, K1.
**Next row** K2tog, K2tog tbl. 2 sts.
**Next row** K2tog.
Fasten off.
Make second strap in same way, but using E.

### Front D-ring sections (make 2)
Using US 6 (4 mm) needles and D, cast on 1 st.
Work as for front strap from \*\* to \*\*.
Cont in patt until piece measures 6 in/15 cm from cast-on edge, ending with a WS row.
Cast/bind off.
Make second piece in same way, but using E.

### To finish
Fold cast-on end of each main belt around the center of two D rings and sew in position. Repeat this process with front buckle sections. Using the photograph as a guide, slip stitch main straps to jacket and sew front buckle and front straps to the front of jacket in same way.

# 7 Colorful cable coat

Add a splash of color to a dog's life with this multicolored cabled coat. Although it is worked in a light, washable yarn, the coat is thick and warm because of its cabled texture.

### Yarn
1 (2: 2: 2: 3: 3: 4) 1¾ oz/50 g balls of Rowan *All Seasons Cotton* in main shade **A** (pale green/Lime Leaf 217) and one ball each in **B** (pink/Giddy 203), **C** (orange/Cheery 205), **D** (blue/Ravish 199) and **E** (yellow/Citron 216)

### Needles and extras
Pair each of US 6 (4 mm) and US 8 (5 mm) knitting needles
Cable needle
3 (3: 3: 3: 4: 4: 4) x ⅝ in/15 mm diameter buttons
2 press-stud fasteners/snaps

### Tension/Gauge
17 sts and 24 rows to 4 in/10 cm over stocking/stockinette stitch using US 8 (5 mm) needles.

### Sizes and measurements

| | XXS | XS | S | M | L | XL | XXL | |
|---|---|---|---|---|---|---|---|---|
| **To fit chest measuring approximately** | | | | | | | | |
| | 16 | 18 | 20 | 22 | 24 | 26 | 28 | in |
| | 41 | 46 | 51 | 56 | 61 | 67 | 72 | cm |

**Knitted measurements**
**Width across back (excluding edging and strap)**

| 9½ | 10 | 11 | 12 | 13 | 14 | 15½ | in |
|---|---|---|---|---|---|---|---|
| 24 | 26 | 28 | 30 | 33 | 36 | 39 | cm |

**Length (from center back neck edge, excluding neckband)**

| 9 | 10 | 12 | 14 | 15½ | 19 | 19½ | in |
|---|---|---|---|---|---|---|---|
| 23 | 25 | 30 | 35 | 40 | 48 | 50 | cm |

### Abbreviations
**C6B (cable 6 back)** = slip 3 sts on to cable needle and hold at the back of work, knit next 3 sts, knit 3 sts from cable needle.
See page 9 for other abbreviations.

## Coat

Using US 6 (4 mm) needles and D, cast on 40 (44: 48: 52: 56: 60: 66) sts.

Work 2 rows in garter st (knit every row).

Break off B and join in E.

Work 2 rows more in garter st.

Break off E and join in B.

Work 2 rows more in garter st.

Break off B and join in C.

Work 2 rows more in garter st.

Break off C and join in A.

Change to US 8 (5 mm) needles.

Using a separate ball of yarn for each color and twisting yarns tog when changing colors, beg stripes and inc on next row as foll:

**Next row (inc row) (RS)** K2 (4: 6: 4: 6: 4: 7) using A, *[K1, M1, K1] once using B, [K1, M1, K1] once using E, K4 using A, [K1, M1, K1] once using D, [K1, M1, K1] once using C, K4 using A, rep from * to last 6 (8: 10: 0: 2: 8: 11) sts, [K1, M1, K1] 1 (1: 1: 0: 0: 1: 1) time using B, [K1, M1, K1] 1 (1: 1: 0: 0: 1: 1) time using E, K2 (4: 6: 0: 2: 4: 7) using A. 50 (54: 58: 64: 68: 74: 80) sts.

Using colors as set by last row, purl 1 row.

Using colors as set throughout, beg cable patt as foll:

**Patt row 1 (RS)** K2 (4: 6: 4: 6: 4: 7), * C6B, K4, rep from * to last 8 (0: 2: 0: 2: 0: 1) sts, C6B 1 (0: 0: 0: 0: 0: 0) times, K2 (0: 2: 0: 2: 0: 1).

**Patt rows 2–6** Beg with a P row, work 5 rows in st st.

Last 6 rows are repeated in colors as set to form patt.

Cont in patt as set until coat measures 9 (10: 12: 14: 15½: 19: 19½) in/23 (25: 30: 35: 40: 48: 50) cm from cast-on edge, ending with a WS row.

**Shape neck**

Keeping patt correct throughout, cont as foll:

**Next row** Patt 22 (23: 25: 27: 29: 31: 33), then turn, leaving rem sts on a holder.

Cast/bind off 3 sts at beg of next row. 19 (20: 22: 24: 26: 28: 30) sts.

Dec 1 st at neck edge of next 3 rows. 16 (17: 19: 21: 23: 25: 27) sts.

Work 1 row.

Dec 1 st at neck edge of next row and foll alt row. 14 (15: 17: 19: 21: 23: 25) sts.

Work 3 rows.

Dec 1 st at neck edge of next row. 13 (14: 16: 18: 20: 22: 24) sts.

Work straight/even until coat measures 14½ (15: 17½: 19½: 22: 26: 27½) in/37 (38: 44: 50: 56: 66: 70) cm from cast-on edge, ending with a WS row.

Change to US 6 (4 mm) needles.

Break off A and join in C.

Work 2 rows in garter st.

Break off C and join in B.

Work 2 rows in garter st.

Break off B and join in E.

Knit 1 row.

**Next row** K2 (3: 4: 4: 1: 2: 3), [K2tog, yf, K6] 1 (1: 1: 1: 2: 2: 2) times, K2tog, yf, K to end.

Knit 1 row.

Break off E and join in D.

Work 2 rows more in garter st.

Cast/bind off.

With RS facing and using US 8 (5 mm) needles, rejoin yarn to rem sts and, keeping patt correct throughout, cast/bind off 6 (8: 8: 10: 10: 12: 14) sts, patt to end. 22 (23: 25: 27: 29: 31: 33) sts.

**Next row** Patt to last 2 sts, P2tog. 21 (22: 24: 26: 28: 30: 32) sts.

Cast/bind off 2 sts at beg of next row. 19 (20: 22: 24: 26: 28: 30) sts.

Dec 1 st at neck edge of next 3 rows. 16 (17: 19: 21: 23:

25: 27) sts.

Work 1 row.

Dec 1 st at neck edge of next row and foll alt row. 14 (15: 17: 19: 21: 23: 25) sts.

Work 3 rows.

Dec 1 st at neck edge of next row. 13 (14: 16: 18: 20: 22: 24) sts.

Work straight/even until coat measures 14½ (15: 17½: 19½: 22: 26: 27½) in/37 (38: 44: 50: 56: 66: 70) cm from cast-on edge, ending with a WS row.

Change to US 6 (4 mm) needles.

Break off A and join in C.

Work 2 rows in garter st.

Break off C and join in B.

Work 2 rows in garter st.

Break off B and join in E.

Work 2 rows in garter st.

Break off E and join in D.

Work 2 rows in garter st.

Cast/bind off.

## Neckband

With RS facing and using US 6 (4 mm) needles and C, pick up and knit 27 (27: 27: 28: 30: 34: 37) sts down right side of neck, 6 (8: 8: 10: 10: 12: 14) sts across back neck, and 27 (27: 27: 28: 30: 34: 37) sts left side of neck. 60 (62: 62: 66: 70: 78: 88) sts.

Knit 1 row.

**Next row** K3, K2tog, yf, K to end.

Break off C and join in B.

Work 2 rows more in garter st.

Cast/bind off.

## Side edgings

### Right side

With RS facing and using US 6 (4 mm) needles and C, pick up and knit 66 (68: 78: 88: 98: 116: 122) sts along the right side of the coat from the cast-on edge to the cast-/bound-off edge.

Break off A and join in C.

Work 2 rows in garter st.

Break off C and join in B.

Work 2 rows in garter st.

Break off B and join in E.

Work 2 rows in garter st.

Break off E and join in D.

Work 2 rows in garter st.

Cast/bind off.

### Left side

With RS facing and using US 6 (4 mm) needles and C, pick up and knit 66 (68: 78: 88: 98: 116: 122) sts along left side of coat from cast-/bound-off edge to cast-on edge.

Break off A and join in C.

Work 2 rows in garter st.

Break off C and join in B.

Work 2 rows in garter st.

Break off B and join in E.

Work 2 rows in garter st.

Break off E and join in D.

Work 2 rows in garter st.

Cast/bind off.

## Strap

Using US 6 (4 mm) needles and A, cast on 8 (8: 8: 10: 10: 12: 12) sts.

**Row 1** *K1, P1, rep from * to end.

**Row 2** *P1, K1, rep from * to end.

Last 2 rows are repeated to form moss/seed st patt.

Work in moss/seed st until the strap measures 8 (8½: 9½: 11: 11½: 12½: 14) in/20 (22: 24: 28: 30: 32: 36) cm from cast-on edge.

Cast/bind off in moss/seed st.

## To finish

Do not press.

Sew the cast-on edge of the strap to the inside of the coat so that it will sit just behind the foreleg. Sew press-stud fasteners/snaps to cast-/bound-off edge of strap and to inside of coat to correspond.

Sew on buttons to correspond with buttonholes.

# Perfect pooch

If your dog is the type that likes to be pampered, the selection of coats in this chapter are just the thing for her. There's Fluffy and Frivolous for the elegant, feminine pooch or Wiggly Stripes for the bolder, more extroverted dog. With their emphasis on stitch detail and trimmings, you are sure to find a design here that's perfect for your pooch.

# 1 Bright and bobbly

This fascinating and playfully textured coat will certainly keep your dog content. Because the contrasting bobbles are sewn on as a finishing touch, it is easier to knit than it looks.

### Yarn
4 (4: 5: 5: 6: 6: 7) 1¾ oz/50 g balls of Rowan *Wool Cotton* in main shade **A** (dark green/Shipshape 955) and one ball each in **B** (red/Rich 911), **C** (blue/Aloof 958), **D** (green/Leaf 946) and E (orange/Pumpkin 962)

### Needles and extras
Pair each of US 3 (3¼ mm) and US 6 (4 mm) knitting needles
4 (4: 4: 4: 5: 5: 5) x ½ in/12 mm diameter buttons
2 press-stud fasteners/snaps

### Tension/Gauge
22 sts and 30 rows to 4 in/10 cm over stocking/ stockinette stitch using US 6 (4 mm) needles

### Sizes and measurements

| XXS | XS | S | M | L | XL | XXL | |
|-----|-----|-----|-----|-----|-----|-----|---|

**To fit chest measuring approximately**

| XXS | XS | S | M | L | XL | XXL | |
|-----|-----|-----|-----|-----|-----|-----|---|
| 16 | 18 | 20 | 22 | 24 | 26 | 28 | in |
| 41 | 46 | 51 | 56 | 61 | 67 | 72 | cm |

**Knitted measurements**
**Width across back (excluding strap)**

| 14 | 15½ | 16½ | 18 | 19½ | 21½ | 22 | in |
|-----|-----|-----|-----|-----|-----|-----|---|
| 35 | 38.5 | 42 | 46 | 49.5 | 53 | 56.5 | cm |

**Length (from center back neck edge, excluding neckband)**

| 8½ | 9½ | 11½ | 14 | 15½ | 17½ | 18 | in |
|-----|-----|-----|-----|-----|-----|-----|---|
| 21 | 24 | 29 | 35 | 39 | 45 | 46 | cm |

### Abbreviations
See page 9 for abbreviations.

## Coat

Using US 3 (3¼ mm) needles and A, cast on 77 (85: 93: 101: 109: 117: 125) sts.

**Row 1** *K1, P1, rep from * to last st, K1.

Last row is repeated to form moss/seed st patt.

Work 7 rows more in moss/seed st.

Change to US 6 (4 mm) needles:

**Patt row 1 (RS)** [K1, P1] 3 times, K to last 6 sts, [P1, K1] 3 times.

**Patt row 2** [K1, P1] 3 times, P to last 6 sts, [P1, K1] 3 times.

**Patt row 3** [K1, P1] 3 times, K4, *P1, K7, rep from * to last 11 sts, P1, K4, [P1, K1] 3 times.

**Patt row 4** Rep patt row 2.

**Patt rows 5–8** Rep patt rows 1 and 2 twice.

**Patt row 9** [K1, P1] 3 times K8, *P1, K7, rep from * to last 15 sts, P1, K8, [P1, K1] 3 times.

**Patt row 10** Rep patt row 2.

**Patt rows 11 and 12** Rep patt rows 1 and 2 once.

Last 12 rows are repeated to form patt (textured panel with 6-st moss/seed st borders).

Cont in patt until coat measures 8½ (9½: 11½: 14: 15½: 17½: 18) in/21 (24: 29: 35: 39: 45: 46) cm from cast-on edge, ending with a WS row.

### Shape neck

Keeping patt correct throughout, cont as foll:

**Next row (RS)** Patt 35 (37: 40: 42: 45: 47: 50), then turn,

leaving rem sts on a holder.

Cast/bind off 3 sts at beg of next row. 32 (34: 37: 39: 42: 44: 47) sts.

Dec 1 st at neck edge of next 4 rows. 28 (30: 33: 35: 38: 40: 43) sts.

Work 1 row.

Dec 1 st at neck edge of next row and foll alt row. 26 (28: 31: 33: 36: 38: 41) sts.

Work straight/even until coat measures 13½ (14½: 16½: 19: 21: 24: 25) in/34 (37: 42: 48: 53: 61: 64) cm from cast-on edge, ending with a WS row.

Change to US 3 (3¼ mm) needles.

**Next row (RS)** *K1, P1, rep from * to last 1 (1: 2: 2: 1: 1: 2) sts, K1, P0 (0: 1: 1: 0: 0: 1).

**Next row** P0 (0: 1: 1: 0: 0: 1), K1, *P1, K1, rep from * to end.

Last 2 rows are repeated to form moss/seed st patt.

Work 2 rows more in moss/seed st.

Keeping moss/seed st correct throughout, cont as foll:

**Buttonhole row (RS)** Patt 4, *work 2tog, yrn/yo patt 7, rep from * to last 4 (6: 9: 2: 5: 7: 1) sts, (yrn/yo, work 2tog) 1 (1: 1: 0: 1: 1: 0) times, patt to end.

Work 3 rows more in moss/seed st.

Cast/bind off in moss/seed st.

With RS facing, rejoin A to rem sts and, keeping patt correct throughout, cast/bind off 7 (11: 13: 17: 19: 23: 25) sts, patt to end. 35 (37: 40: 42: 45: 47: 50) sts.

**Next row (WS)** Patt to last 2 sts, P2tog. 34 (36: 39: 41: 44: 46: 49) sts.

Cast/bind off 2 sts at beg of next row. 32 (34: 37: 39: 42: 44: 47) sts.

Dec 1 st at neck edge of next 5 rows. 27 (29: 32: 34: 37: 39: 42) sts.

Work 1 row.

Dec 1 st at neck edge of next row. 26 (28: 31: 33: 36: 38: 41) sts.

Work straight/even until coat measures 13½ (14½: 16½: 19: 21: 24: 25) in/34 (37: 42: 48: 53: 61: 64) cm from cast-on edge, ending with a WS row.

Change to US 3 (3¼ mm) needles.

**Next row (RS)** K0 (0: 1: 1: 0: 0: 1), *P1, K1, rep from * to end.

**Next row** *K1, P1, rep from * to last 0 (0: 1: 1: 0: 0: 1) sts, K0 (0: 1: 1: 0: 0: 1).

Last 2 rows are repeated to form moss/seed st patt.
Work 6 rows more in moss/seed st.
Cast/bind off in moss/seed st.

## Neckband

Press coat very lightly on WS following instructions on yarn label and avoiding moss/seed st.

With RS facing and using US 3 (3¼ mm) needles and A, pick up and knit 33 (33: 33: 33: 37: 43: 49) sts down right side of neck, 7 (11: 13: 17: 19: 23: 25) sts across back neck, and 33 (33: 33: 33: 37: 43: 49) sts up left side of neck.
73 (77: 79: 83: 93: 109: 123) sts.
**Row 1** *K1, P1, rep from * to last st, K1.
Last row is repeated to form moss/seed st patt.
Work 1 row more in moss/seed st.
Keeping moss/seed st correct throughout, cont as foll:
**Buttonhole row** Patt 2, work 2tog, yrn/yo patt to end.
Work 4 rows more in moss/seed st.
Cast/bind off in moss/seed st.

## Strap

Using US 3 (3¼ mm) needles and A, cast on 17 (17: 17: 19: 19: 21: 21) sts.
Work in moss/seed st as for neckband until strap measures 10½ (12: 13: 14: 14½: 15½: 17) in/27 (30: 33: 35: 37: 40: 43) cm from cast-on edge.
Cast/bind off in moss/seed st.

## Bobbles

You will need approximately 120 bobbles.
Make each bobble as foll:
Using US 6 (4 mm) needles and B, C, D or E, cast on 3 sts, leaving a 4 in/10 cm tail.
**Row 1** Inc in first st, K1, inc in last st.
**Row 2** P to end.
**Row 3** K to end.
**Row 4** P to end.
**Row 5** Sl 1, K1, psso, K1, K2tog.
**Row 6** P3tog.
Fasten off, leaving a 4 in/10 cm tail.
Make approximately 30 bobbles each in B, C, D and E.
(Start sewing on bobbles before you make them all because you may need fewer than recommended.)

## To finish

Using the photograph as a guide, stitch one bobble over each purl stitch in textured panel.
Sew cast-on edge of the strap to the inside of the coat so that it will sit just behind the foreleg. Sew press-stud fasteners/snaps to cast-/bound-off edge of strap and to inside of coat to correspond.
Sew on buttons to correspond with buttonholes.

# 2 Paws for thought

Playful paw prints create a charming pattern across this comfortable tweed coat. For the more sophisticated canine, why not use just one contrasting shade for the paw print motifs?

## Yarn
### Multicolored-paws version
2 (2: 3: 3: 4: 5: 5) 1 oz/25 g balls of Rowan *Yorkshire Tweed 4 ply* in main shade **A** (rust/Glory 273) and one each in **B** (yellow/Butterscotch 272), **C** (blue/Cheerful 271), **D** (green/Graze 286) and **E** (purple/Radiant 276)

### Monocolored-paws version
2 (2: 2: 3: 3: 4: 5) 1 oz/25 g balls of Rowan *Yorkshire Tweed 4 ply* in main shade **A** (brown/Feral 284) and 1 (1: 2: 2: 2: 3: 3) balls in **B** (beige/Barley 264)

## Needles and extras
Pair each of US 2 (2¾ mm) and 3¼ mm (US 3) knitting needles
4 (4: 4: 5: 5: 5: 5) x ½ in/12 mm diameter buttons
2 press-stud fasteners/snaps

## Tension/Gauge
28 sts and 36 rows to 4 in/10 cm over stocking/stockinette stitch using US 3 (3¼ mm) needles.

## Sizes and measurements

| | XXS | XS | S | M | L | XL | XXL | |
|---|---|---|---|---|---|---|---|---|
| **To fit chest measuring approximately** | | | | | | | | |
| | 16 | 18 | 20 | 22 | 24 | 26 | 28 | in |
| | 41 | 46 | 51 | 56 | 61 | 67 | 72 | cm |

**Knitted measurements**
**Width across back (excluding strap)**

| | | | | | | | | |
|---|---|---|---|---|---|---|---|---|
| 12½ | 13½ | 14 | 15 | 16½ | 17¾ | 18½ | in |
| 31.5 | 33.5 | 35.5 | 38 | 42 | 44 | 47 | cm |

**Length (from center back neck edge, excluding neckband)**

| | | | | | | | |
|---|---|---|---|---|---|---|---|
| 11 | 12 | 14 | 15½ | 18 | 21½ | 22 | in |
| 28 | 30.5 | 35.5 | 40 | 46 | 54.5 | 56 | cm |

## Abbreviations
See page 9 for abbreviations.

## Special chart notes
When following chart, work complete motifs only.
For monocolored-paws version, use B for B, C, D and E on chart.

## Coat

Using US 2 (2¾ mm) needles and A, cast on 88 (94: 100: 106: 118: 124: 132) sts.

**Row 1** *K1, P1, rep from * to end.

**Row 2** *P1, K1, rep from * to end.

Last 2 rows are repeated to form moss/seed st patt.

Work 2 rows more in moss/seed st.

Change to US 3 (3¾ mm) needles and, using a separate length of yarn for each area of color, place st st chart patt on next 2 rows as foll:

**Patt row 1** [K1, P1] twice, K80 (86: 92: 98: 110: 116: 124) sts from chart row 1, [K1, P1] twice.

**Patt row 2** [P1, K1] twice, P80 (86: 92: 98: 110: 116: 124) sts from chart row 2, [P1, K1] twice.

Last 2 rows set patt (st st chart patt with 4-st moss/seed st borders).

Cont in patt until coat measures 11 (12: 14: 15½: 18: 21½: 22) in/28 (30.5: 35.5: 40: 46: 54.5: 56) cm from cast-on edge, ending with a WS row.

## Shape neck

Keeping patt correct as set throughout, cont as foll:

**Next row (RS)** Patt 39 (41: 44: 47: 49: 51: 51), then turn, leaving rem sts on a holder.

Cast/bind off 3 sts at beg of next row. 36 (38: 41: 44: 45: 48: 48) sts.

Dec 1 st at neck edge of next 3 rows. 33 (35: 38: 41: 43: 45: 45) sts.

Work 1 row.

Dec 1 st at neck edge of next row and foll 2 alt rows. 30 (32: 35: 38: 40: 42: 42) sts.

Work 3 rows.

Dec 1 st at neck edge of next row and foll 4th row. 28 (32: 33: 36: 37: 40: 40) sts.

Work straight/even until coat measures 16½ (18: 20½: 22½: 25: 25½: 30½) in/42 (45.5: 51.5: 57: 64: 75: 77) cm from cast-on edge, ending with a WS row.

Break off B, C, D and E.

Change to US 2 (2¾ mm) needles and, using A only, cont as foll:

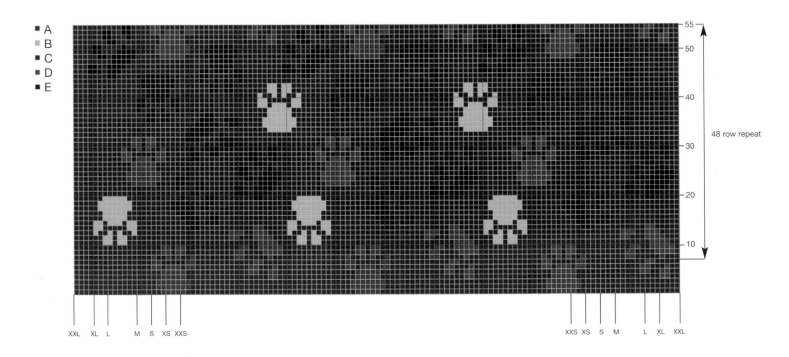

**Next row (RS)** *K1, P1, rep from * to last 0 (0: 1: 0: 0: 0: 0) st, K0 (0: 1: 0: 0: 0: 0: 0).

**Buttonhole row** K0 (0: 1: 0: 0: 0: 0), P1, K1, *K2tog, yf/yo, work 7 sts in moss/seed st, rep from * to last 7 (9: 12: 6: 8: 10: 10) sts, K2tog, yf, work in moss/seed st to end.

**Next row** *K1, P1, rep from * to last 0 (0: 1: 0: 0: 0: 0) st, K0 (0: 1: 0: 0: 0: 0).

**Next row** K0 (0: 1: 0: 0: 0: 0), *P1, K1, rep from * to end. Cast/bind off in moss/seed st.

With RS facing and using US 3 (3¼ mm) needles, rejoin yarn to rem sts and cast/bind off 10 (12: 12: 12: 20: 22: 30) sts, patt to end. 39 (41: 44: 47: 49: 51: 51) sts.

**Next row (WS)** Patt to last 2 sts, P2tog. 38 (40: 43: 46: 48: 50: 50) sts.

Cast/bind off 2 sts at beg of next row. 36 (38: 41: 44: 46: 48: 48) sts.

Dec 1 st at neck edge of next 3 rows. 33 (35: 38: 41: 43: 45: 45) sts.

Work 1 row.

Dec 1 st at neck edge of next row and foll 2 alt rows. 30 (32: 35: 38: 40: 42: 42) sts.

Work 3 rows.

Dec 1 st at neck edge of next row and foll 4th row. 28 (30: 33: 36: 38: 40: 40) sts.

Work straight/even until coat measures 16½ (18: 20½: 22½: 25: 25½: 30½) in/42 (45.5: 51.5: 57: 64: 75: 77) cm from cast-on edge, ending with a WS row.

Break off B, C, D and E.

Change to US 2 (2¾ mm) needles and, using A only, cont as foll:

**Next row (RS)** P0 (0: 0: 0: 1: 0: 0) *K1, P1, rep from * to end.

**Next row** *P1, K1, rep from * to last 0 (0: 0: 0: 1: 0: 0) sts P0 (0: 0: 0: 1: 0: 0).

Rep last 2 rows once more.

Cast/bind off in moss/seed st.

## Neckband

With RS facing and using US 2 (2¾ mm) needles and A, pick up and knit 42 (45: 48: 50: 53: 59: 62) sts down right side of neck, 10 (12: 12: 12: 20: 22: 30) sts across back neck and 42 (45: 48: 50: 53: 59: 62) sts up left side of neck. 92 (102: 108: 112: 126: 130: 154) sts.

**Next row** *K1, P1, rep from * to end.

**Buttonhole row** P1, K1, K2tog, yf/yo *P1, K1, rep from * to end.

**Next row** *K1, P1, rep from * to end.

**Next row** *P1, K1, rep from * to end

Cast/bind off in moss/seed st.

## Strap

Using US 3 (3¼ mm) needles and A, cast on 21 sts.

**Row 1** *K1, P1, rep from * to end.

Last row is repeated to form moss/seed st patt.

Work in moss/seed st until strap measures 8 (8½: 10½: 12½: 13: 13½: 14) in/20 (22: 27: 32: 33: 34: 36) cm.

Cast/bind off in moss/seed st.

## To finish

Sew the cast-on edge of strap to inside of coat so that it will sit just behind the foreleg. Sew press-stud fasteners/snaps to cast-/bound-off edge of strap and to inside of coat to correspond.

Sew on buttons to correspond with buttonholes.

# 3 Fluffy and frivolous

Pink and fluffy, this is just the outfit for the chic pooch to be seen out and about in. You can be sure that heads will turn whenever it is worn. Worked in a chunky yarn, it can be knitted in a flash!

**Yarn**
3 (3: 3: 4: 4) 3½ oz/100 g balls of Rowan *Big Wool* in main shade **A** (pink/Glamour 036) and 2 (2: 3: 3: 3) 50 g/1¾ oz balls of Rowan *Big Wool Tuft* in **B** (pale pink/Powder Puff 061)

**Needles and extras**
Pair each of US 17 (12 mm) and US 19 (15 mm) knitting needles
8 (9: 10: 11: 13) x 1 in/25 mm diameter buttons
3 x 20 (22: 24: 26: 28) in/51 (56: 61: 66: 72) cm lengths of thin round elastic (optional)

**Tension/Gauge**
8 sts and 12 rows to 4 in/10 cm over stocking/stockinette stitch using US 17 (12 mm) needles.

**Sizes and measurements**

| S | M | L | XL | XXL | |
|---|---|---|----|-----|---|

**To fit chest measuring approximately**

| S | M | L | XL | XXL | |
|----|----|----|----|----|-----|
| 20 | 22 | 24 | 26 | 28 | in |
| 51 | 56 | 61 | 67 | 72 | cm |

**Knitted measurements**
**Around chest**

| 23 | 25 | 27 | 29 | 31 | in |
|----|----|----|----|----|-----|
| 59 | 64 | 69 | 74 | 79 | cm |

**Length (from center back neck edge, excluding collar)**

| 15 | 17 | 19 | 22 | 23 | in |
|----|----|----|----|----|-----|
| 38 | 43 | 48 | 56 | 59 | cm |

## Abbreviations
See page 9 for abbreviations.

## Coat

Using US 17 (12 mm) needles and B, cast on 47 (51: 55: 59: 63) sts.

Work 2 rows in garter st (knit every row).

Break off B and join in A.

**Rib row 1** (RS) K3, *P1, K3, rep from * to end.

**Rib row 2** P3, *K1, P3, rep from * to end.

**Rib row 3** *K3, P1, rep from * to last 3 sts, K2tog, yf, K1.

**Rib row 4** Rep row 2.

**Rib rows 5 and 6** Rep rows 1 and 2.

Beg with a K row, work 4 rows in st st.

**Buttonhole row (RS)** K to last 3 sts, K2tog, yf, K1.

Cont in st st, working a buttonhole row on every 8th row until coat measures 10 (12: 14: 17: 18) in/25 (30: 35: 43: 46) cm from cast-on edge, ending with a WS row.

### Divide for leg holes

**Next row (RS)** K18 (20: 22: 24: 26), K2tog, then turn, leaving rem sts on a holder. 19 (21: 23: 25: 27) sts.

Purl 1 row.

**Next row** K to last 2 sts, K2tog. 18 (20: 22: 24: 26) sts.

Rep last 2 rows twice more. 16 (18: 20: 22: 24) sts.

Purl 1 row.

Place these sts on another holder and DO NOT break off yarn but set this ball aside to use later.

With RS facing, join a new ball of A to rem sts on first holder and K4 sts, then turn, leaving rem sts on holder. Working on these 4 sts only, cont in st st and work 7 rows more.

Break off yarn and leave these sts on a holder.

With RS facing, rejoin A to rem 23 (25: 27: 29: 31) sts and, keeping buttonholes correct as set throughout, K2tog tbl, knit to end. 22 (24: 26: 28: 30) sts.

Purl 1 row.

Rep last 2 rows 3 times more. 19 (21: 23: 25: 27) sts.

Break off yarn and leave these sts on a holder.

### Join sections

Slide all sts on to one needle and with RS facing and, using ball of A previously set aside, cont as foll:

**Next row (RS)** K14 (16: 18: 20: 22), K2tog, K4 (from centre gusset), K2tog tbl, K to end. 37 (41: 45: 49: 53) sts.

Purl 1 row.

**Next row** K13 (15: 17: 19: 21), K2tog, K4, K2tog tbl, K to end. 35 (39: 43: 47: 51) sts.

Purl 1 row.

**Next row** K12 (14: 16: 18: 20), K2tog, K4, K2tog tbl, K to end. 33 (37: 41: 45: 49) sts.

Purl 1 row.

**Next row** K11 (13: 15: 17: 19), K2tog, K4, K2tog tbl, K to end. 31 (35: 39: 43: 47) sts.

Purl 1 row.

Cast/bind off.

## Edging

Press coat lightly on WS following instructions on yarn label and avoiding textured areas.

With RS facing, using US 17 (12 mm) needles and B, pick up and knit 32 (36: 40: 46: 50) sts along buttonhole edge.

Knit 1 row.

Cast/bind off.

## Sleeves (both alike)

With RS facing, using US 17 (12 mm) needles and B, cast on 13 sts.

Work 2 rows in garter st.

Break off B and join in A.

**Rib row 1 (RS)** K1, *P1, K3 rep from * to end.

**Rib row 2** *P3, K1, rep from * to last st, P1.

Last 2 rows are repeated to form rib patt.

Cont in rib until sleeve measures 8 in/20 cm from cast-on edge, ending with a WS row.

Cast/bind off loosely in rib.

## Collar

Using US 19 (15 mm) needles and B, cast on 35 (39: 43: 51: 55) sts.

Work 2 rows in garter st.

Break off B and join in A.

**Rib row 1 (RS)** K3, *P1, K3, rep from * to end.

**Rib row 2** *P3, K1, rep from * to last st, P1.

**Rib row 3 (buttonhole row)** K3, *P1, K3, rep from * to last 4 sts, P1, K2tog, yf, K1.

**Rib row 4** Rep rib row 2.

**Rib row 5** Rep rib row 1.

Last 2 rows are repeated to form rib patt.

Cont in rib, working a buttonhole row on every 8th row, until collar measures 6 in/15 cm from cast-on edge.

Change to US 17 (12 mm) needles.

Cont in rib until collar measures 10 in/25 cm from cast-on edge.

Cast/bind off loosely in rib.

## Collar edging

Using US 17 (12 mm) needles and B, pick up and knit 20 sts along buttonhole edge of collar.

Knit 1 row.

Cast/bind off.

## To finish

Sew sleeve seams. Sew sleeves into leg holes. Sew collar to neck edge. If necessary for fit, thread lengths of elastic through WS of rib section of coat and secure at buttonhole and button-band edges.

Sew on buttons to correspond with buttonholes.

# 4 Mesh coat

This little mesh number is bound to catch the eye when it's paraded by its proud owner, whether in the park, the city streets or on the beach. It is just the thing for a balmy summer evening.

**Yarn**
1 (2: 2: 2: 2: 2: 3) 1¾ oz/50 g balls of Rowan *4 ply Cotton* in bright pink/Cheeky 133

**Needles and extras**
Pair of US 3 (3¼ mm) knitting needles
5 x ⅝ in/15 mm diameter buttons

**Tension/Gauge**
27 sts and 25 rows to 4 in/10 cm over mesh pattern using US 3 (3¼ mm) needles.

**Abbreviations**
See page 9 for abbreviations.

**Sizes and measurements**

| XXS | XS | S | M | L | XL | XXL | |
|---|---|---|---|---|---|---|---|
| **To fit chest measuring approximately** | | | | | | | |
| 16 | 18 | 20 | 22 | 24 | 26 | 28 | in |
| 41 | 46 | 51 | 56 | 61 | 67 | 72 | cm |

**Knitted measurements**
**Width across back (excluding strap)**

| XXS | XS | S | M | L | XL | XXL | |
|---|---|---|---|---|---|---|---|
| 12 | 12½ | 14 | 15½ | 16½ | 18 | 19½ | in |
| 30 | 32 | 35.5 | 39 | 42 | 45.5 | 49 | cm |

**Length (from center back neck edge)**

| XXS | XS | S | M | L | XL | XXL | |
|---|---|---|---|---|---|---|---|
| 6½ | 7 | 8 | 9 | 11 | 12 | 13½ | in |
| 16 | 18 | 20 | 23 | 28 | 31 | 34 | cm |

## Coat

Using US 3 (3¼ mm) needles, cast on 69 (75: 84: 93: 102: 111: 120) sts.

**Patt row 1 (RS)** K2, * sl 2, pass first slipped st over 2nd slipped st and off needle, sl 1, pass 2nd slipped st over 3rd and off needle, slip 3rd slipped st back on to left needle, yf/yo twice, K 3rd slipped st, rep from * to last st, K1.

**Patt row 2** K3, *P1, K2, rep from * to end. 69 (75: 84: 93: 102: 111: 120) sts.

Last 2 rows are repeated to form patt.

Taking extra sts into patt and keeping patt correct throughout, cont in patt as foll:

Cast on 3 sts at beg on next 4 rows. 81 (87: 96: 105: 114: 123: 126) sts.

Work straight/even until coat measures 6½ (7: 8: 9: 11: 12: 13½) in/16 (18: 20: 23: 28: 31: 34) cm from cast-on edge, ending with a WS row.

### Shape neck

Keeping patt correct throughout, cont as foll:

**Next row (RS)** Patt 32 (32: 38: 38: 41: 44: 47), then turn, leaving rem sts on a holder.

Cast/bind off 3 sts at beg of next row. 29 (29: 35: 35: 38: 41: 44) sts.

Dec 1 st at neck edge of next 3 rows. 26 (26: 32: 32: 35: 38: 41) sts.

Work 1 row.

Dec 1 st at neck edge of next row and foll alt row. 24 (24: 30: 30: 33: 36: 39) sts.

Work straight/even until coat measures 11 (12: 13½: 15: 15½: 17½: 18) in/28 (30: 34: 38: 40: 44: 46) cm from cast-on edge, ending with a WS row.

Cast/bind off 3 sts at beg of next row. 21 (21: 27: 27: 30: 33: 36) sts.

Work 1 row.

Cast/bind off 3 sts at beg of next row. 18 (18: 24: 24: 27: 30: 33) sts.

Work 1 row

Cast/bind off.

With RS facing, rejoin yarn to rem sts and, keeping patt correct throughout, cast/bind off 17 (23: 20: 29: 32: 35: 38) sts, patt to end. 32 (32: 38: 38: 41: 44: 47) sts.

Work 1 row.

Cast/bind off 3 sts at beg of next row. 29 (29: 35: 35: 38: 41: 44) sts.

Dec 1 st at neck edge of next 3 rows. 26 (26: 32: 32: 35: 38: 41) sts.

Work 1 row.

Dec 1 st at neck edge of next row and foll alt row. 24 (24: 30: 30: 33: 36: 39) sts.

Work straight/even until coat measures 11 (12: 13½: 15: 15½: 17½: 18) in/28 (30: 34: 38: 40: 44: 46) cm from cast-on edge, ending with a RS row.

Cast/bind off 3 sts at beg of next row. 21 (21: 27: 27: 30: 33: 36) sts.

Work 1 row.

Cast/bind off 3 sts at beg of next row. 18 (18: 24: 24: 27: 30: 33) sts.

Work 1 row.

Cast/bind off.

## Strap

Using US 3 (3¼ mm)needles, cast on 18 sts.

Work in patt as for coat until strap measures 5½ (6½: 8: 8½: 9½: 10½: 12) in/14 (17: 20: 22: 24: 27: 30) cm from cast-on edge, ending with a RS row.

Cast/bind off on WS in patt.

## To finish

Do not press.

Sew one button to each corner of strap and one to right front neck.

Use appropriate spaces in the mesh (instead of buttonholes) to fasten the buttons.

# 5 Wiggly stripes

The striking wiggly stripes on this vibrant black and red tweed coat are perfect for the bolder, more extroverted dog. The simple back fastening will make dressing your four-legged friend quick and easy.

**Yarn**
1 (1: 1: 2: 2: 3: 3) 1¾ oz/50 g balls of Rowan *Tweed DK* in main shade **A** (red/Scarlet 344) and 1 (1: 1: 2: 2: 3: 3) balls in **B** (black/Top Hat 351)

**Needles and extras**
Pair each of US 3 (3¼ mm) and US 6 (4 mm) knitting needles
4 (4: 5: 5: 6: 6: 7) x ⅝ in/15 mm diameter buttons

**Tension/Gauge**
22 sts and 30 rows to 4 in/10 cm over stocking/stockinette stitch using US 6 (4 mm) needles.

**Abbreviations**
See page 9 for abbreviations.

**Sizes and measurements**

| | XXS | XS | S | M | L | XL | XXL | |
|---|---|---|---|---|---|---|---|---|
| **To fit chest measuring approximately** | | | | | | | | |
| | 16 | 18 | 20 | 22 | 24 | 26 | 28 | in |
| | 41 | 46 | 51 | 56 | 61 | 67 | 72 | cm |
| **Knitted measurements** **Around chest** | | | | | | | | |
| | 17½ | 19 | 21 | 23 | 25 | 27 | 28½ | in |
| | 44 | 47.5 | 53.5 | 58.5 | 64 | 68 | 73 | cm |
| **Length (from center back neck, excluding neckband)** | | | | | | | | |
| | 7½ | 7¾ | 9½ | 11 | 13 | 13¼ | 13¾ | in |
| | 19 | 20 | 24.5 | 28 | 33 | 33.5 | 35 | cm |

## Coat

Using US 3 (3¼ mm) needles and A, cast on 88 (100: 112: 124: 132: 144: 156) sts.

**Rib row 1 (RS)** K1, *P2, K2, rep from * to last 3 sts, P2, K1.

**Rib row 2** P1, *K2, P2, rep from * to last 3 sts, K2, P1.

Last 2 rows are repeated to form rib patt.

Work 7 rows more in rib, so ending with a RS row.

**Size XXS only:**

**Next row (inc row) (WS)** Rib 17, M1, [rib 18, M1] 3 times, rib to end. 92 sts.

**Sizes S and XL only:**

**Next row (inc row) (WS)** Rib 50 (66: 72), M1, rib to end. 113 (133: 145) sts.

**Size L only:**

**Next row (inc row) (WS)** [Rib 22, M1] 5 times, rib to end. 137 sts.

**Sizes XS, M and XXL only:**

Work 1 row more in rib, so ending with a WS row.

**All sizes:**

Change to US 6 (4 mm) needles.

Place st st chart patt on next row as foll:

**Patt row 1 (RS)** K1 (5: 4: 2: 1: 5: 3) using A, work chart row 1 working 15-st repeat 6 (6: 7: 8: 9: 9: 10) times, K to end using A.

Beg with a P row, cont in st st, foll chart as set and rep chart 20-row repeat as necessary, until coat measures

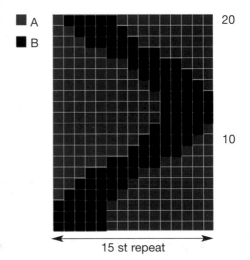

■ A
■ B

20

10

← 15 st repeat →

5 (5½: 6½: 7½: 8½: 9½: 10) in/13 (14: 16: 19: 21: 24: 26) cm from cast-on edge, ending with a WS row.

**Divide for leg holes**

Keeping chart patt correct as set throughout, cont as foll:

**Next row (RS)** Patt 38 (41: 45: 49: 53: 56: 60), K2tog tbl, then turn, leaving rem sts on a holder.

Working on these 39 (42: 46: 50: 53: 57: 61) sts only, cont as foll:

Work 1 row.

**Next row** Patt to last 2 sts, K2tog tbl. 38 (41: 45: 49: 53: 56: 60) sts.

**Sizes S, M, L, XL and XXL only:**

Rep last 2 rows twice more. 43 (47: 51: 54: 58) sts.

Work 3 rows.

**Sizes M, L, XL and XXL only:**

**Next row** Patt to last 2 sts, K2tog tbl. 46 (50: 53: 57) sts.

**Sizes L, XL and XXL only:**

Work 3 rows.

**Next row** Patt to last 2 sts, K2tog tbl. 49 (52: 56) sts.

Work 5 rows.

**Sizes XL and XXL only:**

**Next row** Patt to last 2 sts, K2tog tbl. 51 (55) sts.

**Sizes XXS, XS, S and M only:**

Work 6 rows.

**Sizes XXS, XS, M, XL and XXL only:**

Work 1 row.

All sizes end with a WS row. 38 (41: 43: 46: 49: 51: 55) sts.

**All sizes:**

Work 1 row.

Place these sts on another holder and DO NOT break off yarn but set this ball aside to use later.

With RS facing, join a new ball of yarn at first leg divide on first holder and, keeping patt correct throughout, K2tog, patt 8 (10: 15: 18: 23: 25: 28), K2tog tbl, turn, leaving rem sts on holder. 10 (12: 17: 20: 25: 27: 30) sts.

Work 1 row.

**Next row (RS)** K2tog, work to last 2 sts, K2tog tbl. 8 (10: 15: 18: 23: 25: 28) sts.

**Sizes S, M, L, XL and XXL only:**

Rep last 2 rows twice more. 11 (14: 19: 21: 24) sts.

Work 3 rows.

**Sizes M, L, XL and XXL only:**

**Next row** K2tog, patt to last 2 sts, K2tog tbl. 12 (17: 19: 22) sts.

**Sizes L, XL and XXL only:**
Work 3 rows.
**Next row** K2tog, patt to last 2 sts, K2tog tbl. 15 (17: 20) sts.
Work 5 rows.
**Sizes XL and XXL only:**
**Next row** K2tog, Work to last 2 sts, K2tog tbl. 15 (18) sts.
**Sizes XXS, XS, S and M only:**
Work 6 rows.
**Sizes XXS, XS, M, XL and XXL only:**
Work 1 row.
All sizes end with a WS row. 8 (10: 11: 12: 15: 15: 18) sts.
**All sizes:**
Work 1 row.
Break off yarn and place these sts on another holder.
With RS facing, rejoin yarn to rem sts on first holder and, keeping patt correct throughout, K2tog, patt to end.
Working on these 39 (42: 46: 50: 54: 57: 61) sts, cont as foll:
Work 1 row.
**Next row (RS)** K2tog, work to end. 38 (41: 45: 59: 53: 56: 60) sts.
**Sizes S, M, L, XL and XXL only:**
Rep last 2 rows twice more. 43 (47: 51: 54: 58) sts.
Work 3 rows.
**Sizes M, L, XL and XXL only:**
**Next row** K2tog, patt to end. 46 (50: 53: 57) sts.
**Sizes L, XL and XXL only:**
Work 3 rows.
**Next row** K2tog, patt to end. 49 (52: 56) sts.
Work 5 rows.
**Sizes XL and XXL only:**
**Next row** K2tog, patt to end. 51 (55) sts.
**Sizes XXS, XS, S and M only:**
Work 6 rows.
**Sizes XXS, XS, M, XL and XXL only:**
Work 1 row.
All sizes end with a WS row. 38 (41: 43: 46: 49: 51: 55) sts.
**All sizes:**
**Join sections**
Slide all sts on to one needle, and with RS facing, using ball of yarn set aside previously and keeping patt correct throughout, cont as foll:

**Sizes S, L and XL only:**
**Next row** Patt 48 (56: 58), K2tog, patt to end. 96 (112: 116) sts.
**All sizes:**
Work 6 (8: 7: 10: 11: 11: 14) rows in patt, so ending with a WS row.

## Neckband

Break off yarn B and cont with A only.
Change to US 3 (3¼ mm) needles.
**Rib row 1** K1, *P2, K2, rep from * to last 3 sts, P2, K1.
**Rib row 2** P1, * K2, P2, rep from * to last 3 sts, P2, K1.
Last 2 rows are repeated to form rib patt.
Work 8 rows more in rib.
Cast/bind off in rib.

## Buttonband

With RS facing and using US 3 (3¼ mm) needles and A, pick up and knit 44 (48: 56: 64: 76: 80: 84) sts from neck edge to cast-on edge of right side.
**Rib row 1** K1, *P2, K2, rep from * to last 3 sts, P2, K1.
**Rib row 2** P1, * K2, P2, rep from * to last 3 sts, P2, K1.
Last 2 rows are repeated to form rib patt.
Work 4 rows more in rib.
Cast/bind off in rib.
Mark positions for 4 (4: 5: 5: 6: 6: 7) buttons along button band.

## Buttonhole band

Press coat lightly on WS following instructions on yarn label and avoiding ribbing.
With RS facing and using US 3 (3¼ mm) needles and A, pick up and knit 44 (48: 56: 64: 76: 80: 84) sts from neck edge to cast-on edge of right side.
Work 2 rows in rib as for buttonband.
**Buttonhole row** Keeping rib correct, work in rib while working buttonholes to correspond with positions marked on buttonband as foll: work 2tog, yrn/yo twice, work 2tog.
**Next row** Work in rib as set, working [K1, P1] into each double yrn/yo of previous row.
Work 2 rows more in rib.
Cast/bind off in rib.

## To finish

Sew on buttons to correspond with buttonholes.

# 6 Pucker up

Striking and bold, this eye-catching coat will ensure the dog-about-town is seen by all the right people. Don't be put off by the complex-looking design, it's actually a very easy slip-stitch pattern.

## Yarn
2 (2: 3: 3: 3: 4: 5) 1 oz/25 g balls of Rowan *Tweed 4 ply* in main shade **A** (yellow/Butterscotch 272) and 2 (2: 3: 3: 3: 4: 5) balls in **B** (dark green/Lustre 282)

## Needles and extras
Pair each of US 2 (2¾ mm) and US 3 (3¼ mm) knitting needles
4 (4: 4: 5: 5: 5: 5) x ½ in/13 mm diameter buttons
2 press-stud fasteners/snaps

## Tension/Gauge
28 sts and 36 rows to 4 in/10 cm over stocking/stockinette stitch using US 3 (3¼ mm) needles.

## Abbreviations
See page 9 for abbreviations.

## Special note
When working stripes, strand yarns loosely up the side of the work between stripes.

## Sizes and measurements

| XXS | XS | S | M | L | XL | XXL | |
|---|---|---|---|---|---|---|---|

**To fit chest measuring approximately**

| XXS | XS | S | M | L | XL | XXL | |
|---|---|---|---|---|---|---|---|
| 16 | 18 | 20 | 22 | 24 | 26 | 28 | in |
| 41 | 46 | 51 | 56 | 61 | 67 | 72 | cm |

**Knitted measurements**
**Width across back (excluding edging and strap) approximately**

| XXS | XS | S | M | L | XL | XXL | |
|---|---|---|---|---|---|---|---|
| 12 | 13½ | 16 | 17 | 18½ | 18½ | 19½ | in |
| 30.5 | 34 | 40.5 | 42.5 | 47 | 47 | 49 | cm |

**Length (from center back neck edge, excluding neck edging)**

| XXS | XS | S | M | L | XL | XXL | |
|---|---|---|---|---|---|---|---|
| 9 | 10 | 12 | 14 | 15½ | 19 | 20 | in |
| 23 | 25 | 30 | 36 | 40 | 48 | 5 | cm |

## Coat

Using US 2 (2¾ mm) needles and A, cast on 106 (116: 137: 143: 155: 158: 165) sts.

Work 14 rows in garter st (knit every row) in stripes as foll:

[Work 2 rows in B, 2 rows in A] 3 times, then work 2 rows in B.

Change to 3¼ mm (US 3) needles.

**Patt row 1 (RS)** Using A, [K1, sl 1] 5 times, *K10 (12: 12: 13: 15: 12: 13), sl 1, [K1, sl 1] 4 times, rep from * to last st, K1.

**Patt row 2** Using A, [P1, sl 1] 5 times, *P10 (12: 12: 13: 15: 12: 13), sl 1, [P1, sl 1] 4 times, rep from * to last st, P1.

**Patt row 3** Using B, K2, sl 1, [K1, sl 1] 3 times, *K12 (14: 14: 15: 17: 14: 15), sl 1, [K1, sl 1] 3 times, rep from * to last 2 sts, K2.

**Patt row 4** Using B, P2, sl 1, [P1, sl 1] 3 times, *P12 (14: 14: 15: 17: 14: 15), sl 1, [P1, sl 1] 3 times, rep from * to last 2 sts, P2.

Last 4 patt rows are repeated to form slip-stitch patt.

Cont in patt until work measures 9 (10: 12: 14: 15½: 19: 20) in/23 (25: 30: 36: 40: 48: 51) cm from cast-on edge, ending with a WS row.

### Shape neck

Keeping patt correct throughout, cont as foll:

**Next row (RS)** Patt 50 (54: 63: 65: 70: 70: 73), then turn, leaving rem sts on a holder.

Cast/bind off 3 sts at beg of next row. 47 (51: 60: 62: 67: 67: 70) sts.

Dec 1 st at neck edge of next 6 rows. 41 (45: 54: 56: 61: 61: 64) sts.

Work 1 row.

Dec 1 st at neck edge of next row and foll 2 alt rows. 38 (41: 51: 53: 58: 58: 61) sts.

Work straight/even until coat measures 15 (15½: 19: 20: 22½: 26: 28½) in/38 (40:45: 51: 57: 67: 73) cm from cast-on edge, ending with WS row.

### Buttonband

Change to US 2 (2¾ mm) needles.

Work 15 rows in garter st in stripes as foll:

[Work 2 rows in B, 2 rows in A] 3 times, then work 2 rows in B and 1 row in A.

Cast/bind off on WS.

Mark positions for 4 (4: 4: 5: 5: 5: 5) buttons evenly spaced along buttonband.

With RS facing and using US 3 (3¼ mm) needles, rejoin yarn to rem sts and, keeping pattern correct throughout, cast/bind off 6 (8: 11: 13: 15: 18: 19) sts, patt to end. 50 (54: 63: 65: 70: 70: 73) sts.

**Next row (WS)** Patt to last 2 sts, P2tog. 49 (53: 62: 64: 69: 69: 72) sts.

Cast/bind off 2 sts at beg of next row. 47 (51: 60: 62: 67: 67: 70) sts.

Dec 1 st at neck edge of next 6 rows. 41 (45: 54: 56: 61: 61: 64) sts.

Work 1 row.

Dec 1 st at neck edge of next row and foll 2 alt rows. 38 (41: 51: 53: 58: 58: 61) sts.

Work straight/even until coat measures 15 (15½: 19: 20: 22½: 26: 28½) in/38 (40: 45: 51: 57: 67: 73) cm from cast-on edge, ending with a WS row.

### Buttonhole band

Change to US 2 (2¾ mm) needles.

Work 7 rows in garter st in stripes as foll:

Work 2 rows in B, 2 rows in A, 2 rows in B and 1 row in A.

**Buttonhole row 1** Using A, K to end while casting/binding off 2 sts at each point marked for buttonholes.

**Buttonhole row 2** Using B, K to end while casting on 2 sts over those cast/bound off on previous row.

Cont in garter st, work 6 rows more in stripes as foll:

Work 1 row in B, 2 rows in A, 2 rows in B and 1 row in A.

Cast/bind off on WS.

## Neck edging

With RS facing and using US 2 (2¾ mm) needles and B, pick up and knit 48 (50: 52: 54: 58: 64: 70) sts down right side of neck, 6 (8: 11: 13: 15: 18: 19) sts across back neck and 48 (50: 52: 54: 58: 64: 70) sts up left side of neck. 102 (108: 115: 121: 131: 146: 159) sts.

Cast/bind off on WS.

## Side edgings

### Right side

With RS facing and using US 2 (2¾ mm) needles and B, pick up and knit 120 (126: 134: 157: 174: 202: 218) sts up right side of coat.

Cast/bind off on WS.

### Left side

With RS facing and using US 2 (2¾ mm) needles and B, pick up and knit 120 (126: 134: 157: 174: 202: 218) sts down left side of coat.
Cast/bind off on WS.

### Strap

Using US 3 (3¼ mm) needles and A, cast on 21 sts.
Work 4 rows in garter st in stripes as foll:
Work 2 rows in A and 2 rows in B.
Last 4 rows are repeated to form garter st stripe patt.
Stranding yarn loosely up side of work, cont in stripe patt until strap measures 28 (8½: 10½: 12½: 13: 13½: 14) in/20 (22: 27: 32: 33: 34: 36) cm/ from cast-on edge.
Cast/bind off.

### To finish

Do not press.
Sew the cast-on edge of the strap to the inside of the coat so that it will sit just behind the foreleg. Sew press-stud fasteners/snaps to cast-/bound-off edge of strap and to inside of coat to correspond.
Sew on buttons to correspond with buttonholes.

# 7 Pretty in pink

Understated yet feminine, this delightful cardigan will make your pooch feel pampered in pink. The luxury cashmere-mix yarn is very gentle on the fur and is sure to make your dog feel special.

**Yarn**
3 (3: 3: 4: 4: 5: 5) 1¾ oz/50 g balls of RYC *Cashsoft Aran* in main colour **A** (pink/Oat 00001) and one ball in **B** (lilac/Foxglove 00002)

**Needles and extras**
Pair each of US 6 (4 mm) and US 7 (4½ mm) knitting needles
5 (5: 5: 5: 6: 7: 7) x ¾ in/20 mm diameter buttons

**Tension/Gauge**
19 sts and 25 rows to 4 in/10 cm over stocking/stockinette stitch using US 7 (4½ mm) needles.

**Abbreviations**
**tuck5/6/7** = insert right needle into next st as if to knit then through back of loop of same st 5/6/7 rows below and knit 2 sts together.
See page 9 for other abbreviations.

**Sizes and measurements**

| XXS | XS | S | M | L | XL | XXL | |
|---|---|---|---|---|---|---|---|

**To fit chest measuring approximately**

| 16 | 18 | 20 | 22 | 24 | 26 | 28 | in |
|---|---|---|---|---|---|---|---|
| 41 | 46 | 51 | 56 | 60 | 67 | 72 | cm |

**Knitted measurements**
**Around chest**

| 17¾ | 19¼ | 22 | 23½ | 26 | 27¾ | 30¼ | in |
|---|---|---|---|---|---|---|---|
| 44 | 48.5 | 54.5 | 59 | 65 | 70 | 76 | cm |

**Length (from center back neck edge, excluding neckband)**

| 6½ | 7¼ | 9¾ | 12 | 14½ | 17½ | 19 | in |
|---|---|---|---|---|---|---|---|
| 16.5 | 18.5 | 24.5 | 30 | 37 | 45 | 49 | cm |

## Cardigan

Using US 6 (4 mm) needles and B, cast on 84 (92: 104: 112: 124: 132: 144) sts.

Break off B and join in A.

**Rib row 1** K1, *P2, K2, rep from * to last 3 sts, P2, K1.

**Rib row 2** P1, * K2, P2, rep from * to last 3 sts, K2, P1.

Last 2 rows are repeated to form rib patt.

Work 6 rows more in rib.

Change to US 7 (4½ mm) needles.

Beg with a K row, work 12 rows in st st.

**Tuck row 1 (RS)** K2 (10: 2: 10: 2: 10: 2), * tuck5, K1, tuck6, K1, tuck7, K1, tuck7, K1, tuck7, K1, tuck6, K1, tuck5, K7, rep from * to last 2 sts, K2.

Beg with a P row, work 9 rows in st st.

**Tuck row 2 (RS)** K12 (2: 12: 2: 12: 2: 12), *tuck5, K1, tuck6, K1, tuck7, K1, tuck7, K1, tuck7, K1, tuck6, K1, tuck5, K7, rep from * to last 12 (10: 12: 10: 12: 10: 12) sts, K12 (10: 12: 10: 12: 10: 12).

Beg with a P row, work 9 rows in st st, then work tuck row 1 once more.

Beg with a P row, cont in st st until cardigan measures 4¼ (5: 7: 9: 12: 15: 16½) in/11 (13: 18: 23: 30: 38: 42) cm from cast-on edge, ending with a WS row.

### Divide for leg holes

**Next row (RS)** K33 (36: 41: 44: 49: 52: 57), then turn, leaving rem sts on a holder.

Working on these 33 (36: 41: 44: 49: 52: 57) sts only and beg with a P row, work 14 (14: 16: 18: 18: 18: 18) rows in st st.

Place these sts on another holder and DO NOT break off yarn but set this ball aside to use later.

With RS facing, join a new ball of yarn at first leg divide on first holder and K2tog, K14 (16: 18: 20: 22: 24: 26), K2tog tbl, turn, leaving rem sts on a holder. 16 (18: 20: 22: 24: 26: 28) sts.

Purl 1 row.

**Next row (RS)** K2tog, K to last 2 sts, K2tog tbl. 14 (16: 18: 20: 22: 24: 26) sts.

Beg with a P row, work 3 rows in st st.

**Next row (RS)** K2tog, K to last 2 sts, K2tog tbl. 12 (14: 16: 18: 20: 22: 24) sts.

Beg with a P row, work 5 rows in st st.

**Next row (RS)** K2tog, K to last 2 sts, K2tog tbl. 10 (12: 14: 16: 18: 20: 22) sts.

Beg with a P row, work 1 (1: 3: 5: 5: 5: 5) rows in st st.

Break off yarn and place these sts on a 2nd holder.

With RS facing, rejoin yarn to rem sts on first holder and knit to end.

Beg with a P row, work 14 (14: 16: 18: 18: 18: 18) rows in st st.

### Join sections

Slide all sts on to one needle, and with RS facing and using ball of yarn set aside previously, cont as foll:

**Next row (RS)** K across all sts. 76 (84: 96: 100: 116: 124: 136) sts.

Beg with a P row, work 7 (7: 9: 11: 11: 11: 11) rows in st st.

## Neckband

Change to US 6 (4 mm) needles.

**Rib row 1** K1, *P2, K2, rep from * to last 3 sts, P2, K1.

**Rib row 2** P1, * K2, P2, rep from * to last 3 sts, P2, K1.

Last 2 rows are repeated to form rib patt.

Work 6 rows more in rib.

Break off A.

Using B, cast/bind off in rib.

## Buttonband

With RS facing and using US 6 (4 mm) needles and B,
pick up and knit 36 (44: 56: 68: 76: 92: 100) sts from neck
edge to cast-on edge of right side.

**Rib row 1** K1, *P2, K2, rep from * to last 3 sts, P2, K1.
**Rib row 2** P1, * K2, P2, rep from * to last 3 sts, P2, K1.
Last 2 rows are repeated to form rib patt.
Work 6 rows more in rib.
Cast/bind off in rib.
Mark positions for 5 (5: 5: 5: 6: 7: 7) buttons along
buttonband.

## Buttonhole band

With RS facing and using US 6 (4 mm) needles and B,
pick up and knit 36 (44: 56: 68: 76: 92: 100) sts from neck
edge to cast-on edge of right side.
Work 3 rows in rib as for buttonband.
**Buttonhole row** Keeping rib correct, work in rib while
working buttonholes to correspond with positions marked
on buttonband as foll: work 2tog, yrn twice, work 2tog.
**Next row** Work in rib as set, working [K1, P1] into each
double yrn of previous row.
Work 3 rows more in rib.
Cast/bind off in rib.

## Sleeves (both alike)

Using US 6 (4 mm)needles and B, cast on 38 (38: 42: 46:
46: 46: 46) sts.
Break off B and join in A.
**Rib row 1** K1, *P2, K2, rep from * to last 3 sts, P2, K1.
**Rib row 2** P1, * K2, P2, rep from * to last 3 sts, P2, K1.
Last 2 rows are repeated to form rib patt.
Work in rib until sleeve measures 3¼ in/8 cm from cast-
on edge, ending with a rib row 2.
Cast/bind off in rib.

## To finish

Sew together row ends of sleeves. Sew cast-/bound-off
edge of sleeves into leg holes, positioning the sleeve
seams at beginning of leg divisions.
Sew on buttons to correspond with buttonholes.

# Knitting information

Whether you have chosen a simple
but stylish coat for your dog or a more
challenging pattern, this chapter provides
you with all the information you need to
complete it. There are invaluable knitting
tips, ranging from the very basic to the more
complex. There is also information on
choosing a yarn and knitting from a chart,
and finishing techniques that will make all
the difference to the completed coat.

# Holding the needles

Before you cast on, get used to holding the yarn and the needles. They will feel awkward at first, but the more you try, the easier it will get. Don't forget to move your arms and your elbows when you knit – if you only move your wrists, you will find knitting really difficult. It is important to relax when you are knitting. If you are tense and sitting uncomfortably, it will show in your knitting, no matter how expert you become.

**1** The right needle is held in the same way as a pencil. When casting on and working the first few rows, the knitted piece rests between the thumb and the index finger. As the knitting grows, let the thumb slide under the knitted piece and hold the needle from below.

**2** The left needle is held lightly over the top. The thumb and index finger control the tip of the needle.

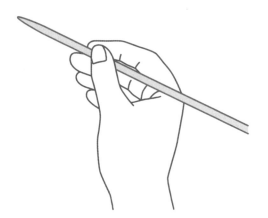

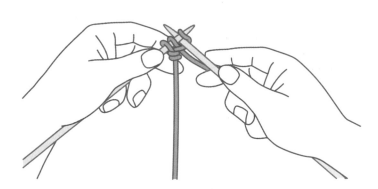

# Holding the yarn

There are many ways of holding the yarn in the right hand. The way shown below is the one most commonly used, but as you get more experienced with knitting, you will find out for yourself which is the best method for you.

The only thing you need to bear in mind when it comes to holding the yarn is that the yarn needs to be able to move easily through your fingers and hand without getting tied up or caught. If this happens, the evenness of your knitting will suffer and you will never obtain the right tension.

Pass the yarn under your little finger, over your third finger, under your middle finger and over your index finger. The index finger is used to pass the yarn around the tip of the left needle when knitting. The tension and flow of the yarn are controlled by gripping the yarn in the crook of the little finger. If you find it difficult to control the tension, pass the yarn around the fingers in the same way, but pass it under and around the little finger before passing it over the third finger. The yarn circled around the little finger will create the tension that keeps the knitting even.

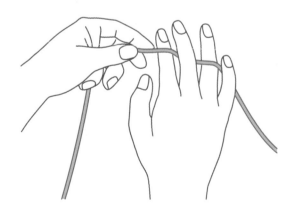

# Casting on

This is the term used to describe making the first row of stitches, which forms the foundation for each piece of knitting. The 'cable cast-on' method described here uses two needles and produces a firm, neat finish. It is important that you achieve an even cast-on row to avoid a wavy edge to your knitting, and this is likely to require some practice.

**1** First, make a slip knot. Wind the yarn around two fingers as shown. Insert a knitting needle over the first strand and under the second strand. Using the needle, pull the strand that is resting on the needle through to the front to form a loop.

**2** Holding the loose ends of the yarn with your left hand, pull the needle upwards, to tighten the knot. Pull the ball end of the yarn again to tighten the knot on the needle.

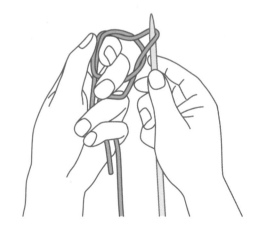

**3** The slip knot should be about 6in/15 cm from the loose end of the yarn: this is now the first stitch. Hold the needle in your left hand.

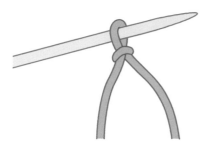

**4** Insert the point of the right-hand needle from front to back through the slip knot. Pass the yarn from the ball end over the point of the right-hand needle.

**5** Bring the point of the right-hand needle with the yarn back through the slip knot, pulling the yarn to make a loop.

**6** Insert the point of the left-hand needle through this loop and remove the right-hand needle, leaving the loop – or second stitch, as it now is – on the left-hand needle. Gently pull the yarn to tighten the stitch.

**7** Insert the point of the right-hand needle between the first and second stitches on the left-hand needle. Wind the yarn over the point of the right-hand needle.

**8** Pull the loop through and place it on the left-hand needle. Repeat steps 7 and 8 until the required number of stitches has been cast on.

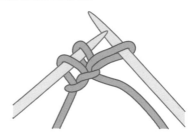

# Knit

The knit stitch is the easiest to learn. If you knit every row, you create garter stitch, which is the simplest of all knitted fabrics. A combination of knit and purl stitches together is the base of most knitted fabrics.

**1** Hold the needle with the cast-on stitches in your left hand and the loose yarn at the back of the work. Insert the point of the right-hand needle from left to right through the front of the first stitch on the left-hand needle.

**2** Pass the yarn from left to right over the point of the right-hand needle.

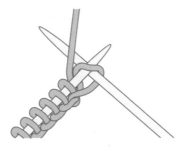

**3** Bring the point of the right-hand needle with the yarn back through the stitch, pulling through a loop, which makes a new stitch on the right-hand needle.

**4** Slip the original stitch off the left-hand needle, keeping the new stitch on the right-hand needle. Pull the yarn end to tighten the stitch on the needle.

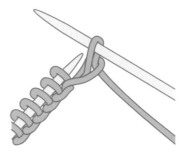

**5** Repeat steps 1–4 once into each of the stitches on the left-hand needle, until all the original stitches have been dropped and all the new stitches are on the right-hand needle. You have now knitted your first row.

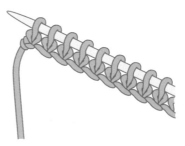

# Purl

The most common fabric knitted is stocking/stockinette stitch, which is created when you knit 1 row, then purl 1 row. Working alternate knit and purl stitches (1 or 2 of each) within a row creates rib, an elastic stitch often used for edgings.

**1** Hold the needle with the cast-on stitches in your left hand, with the loose yarn at the front of the work. Insert the point of the right-hand needle from right to left through the front of the first stitch on the left-hand needle.

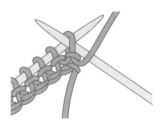

**2** Pass the yarn from right to left over the point of the right-hand needle.

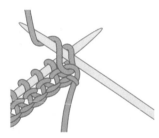

**3** Bring the point of the right-hand needle with the yarn back through the stitch, pulling through a loop, which makes a new stitch on the right-hand needle.

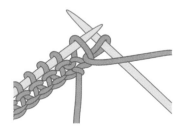

**4** Slip the original stitch off the left-hand needle, keeping the new stitch on the right-hand needle. Pull the yarn end to tighten the stitch on the needle.

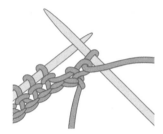

**5** Repeat steps 1–4 once into each of the stitches on the left-hand needle, until all the original stitches have been dropped and all the new stitches are on the right-hand needle. You have now purled one row.

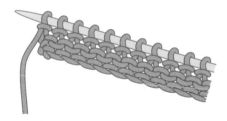

# Increasing

There are a number of methods of increasing the number of stitches in a row. The method described below, called 'make 1' (M1), is used for shaping your knitting.

**Increasing on a knit row**

1  With the right-hand needle, lift the strand of yarn that runs between the stitch you've just knitted and the next one on the left-hand needle.

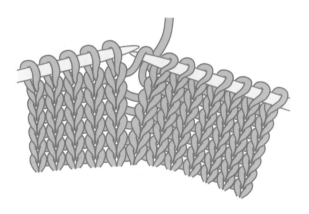

2  Put the strand on to the left-hand needle and then knit it as if it were a normal stitch. This can leave a small hole, so the lifted stitch is usually twisted by working into the back of it, but don't worry if you can't do this.

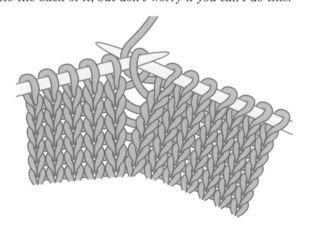

**Increasing on a purl row**

The procedure is exactly the same on a purl row. With the right-hand needle, lift the strand of yarn that runs between the stitch you've just purled and the next one on the left-hand needle. Put the strand on to the left-hand needle and then purl into the back of it by inserting the point of the right-hand needle from back to front. Slip the original loop off the needle.

**Yarn over (yo)**

Another method of increasing used is yarn over (yo). For this increase, the yarn is brought over the needle before working the next stitch, creating an extra loop.

# Decreasing

Decreasing is used in this book mainly to shape the neck and leg openings. In conjunction with a 'yarn over' (see opposite), it is also used to create eyelets (holes) in lace patterns.

### Decreasing on a knit row (K2tog)

Insert the right-hand needle from left to right through two stitches at the same time instead of one, then knit them together as if they were one stitch.

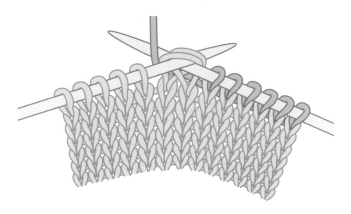

### Decreasing on a purl row (P2tog)

Insert the right-hand needle from right to left through two stitches at the same time instead of one, then purl them together as if they were one stitch.

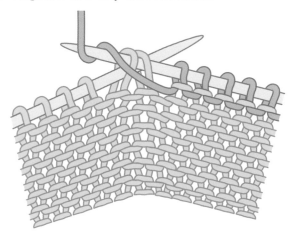

### Slip one, knit one, pass slipped stitch over Sl1, K1, psso

The second method of decreasing used in this book involves a combination of actions. When you come to this abbreviation, first slip the next stitch on to the right-hand needle (sl1), knit the next stitch (K1) and then pass the slipped stitch over the knitted stitch (psso). This makes one stitch from two, which slants to the left.

### Knit two together through the back of loops (K2togtbl)

The third method of decreasing used in this book is a variation on K2tog. Insert the right-hand needle through the back of the next two stitches on the left needle. Take the yarn around the right needle as usual and knit the two stitches together.

# Joining in a new yarn

A new ball of yarn can be joined in on either a right-side or a wrong-side row of your knitting, but to give a neat finish it is important that you always do this at the beginning of the row. This method is also used for working stripes.

To join in a new yarn, simply drop the old yarn, start knitting with the new ball, and then after a few stitches tie the two ends together in a temporary knot. These ends are then sewn into the knitting at the making-up stage (see page 124).

If you are using this method for working stripes when an even number of striped rows is to be knitted do not cut the old yarn – it can be carried up the side of the knitting until you need it again, but make sure you don't pull it too tight or you'll distort your knitting.

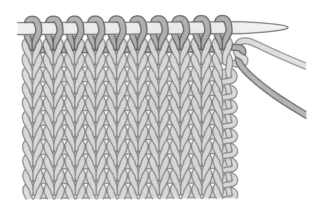

# Casting/binding off

This is the term used to describe securing the stitches at the top of your knitted fabric when you have completed the piece. It is important that the cast-/bound-off edge is elastic, like the rest of your knitting. If you find that your cast-/bind-off is too tight, try using a larger needle. You can cast/bind off knitwise, purlwise or in a combination of stitches, such as rib. The method described below is for casting/binding off knitwise.

**1** Knit the first two stitches as if working a normal knit row. Using the point of the left-hand needle, lift the first stitch over the second stitch and then drop it off the needle. Knit the next stitch and again use the needle point to lift the first stitch over the second stitch. Continue to do this until only one stitch remains on the right-hand needle.

**2** Cut the yarn at least 8 in/20 cm from the stitch, thread the end through the stitch and then slip it off the needle. Draw up the yarn firmly to fasten off.

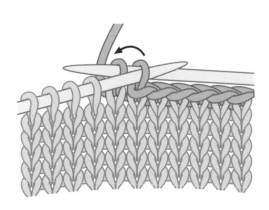

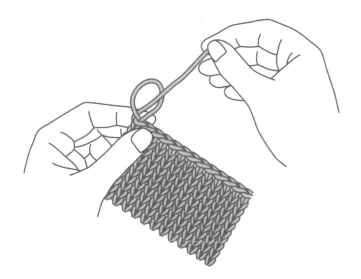

# Finishing techniques

When you have spent many hours knitting, it is essential that you complete your project correctly. Follow the simple instructions provided here to achieve a beautifully finished article.

## Pressing

It is important to press your knitting before making up, to help maintain the shape of the pieces and achieve a professional-looking finish.

With the wrong side of the fabric facing up, pin out each knitted piece on to an ironing board using the measurements given. If specific measurements are not provided for your project, pin out your knitting neatly without overstretching it and unfurl any edges that may be rolling up.

Because each yarn is different, refer to the ball band and press your knitted pieces according to the manufacturer's instructions. Most of the yarns used in this book can be pressed. However, if your yarn contains acrylic, it may not be suitable for pressing. Always use a cloth between the knitting and iron to avoid scorching. Then lightly press or steam the knitted fabric. If you steam your knitting, remember to let it dry completely before removing the pins.

## Sewing in ends

Once you have pressed your finished pieces, you will need to sew in all the loose ends of wool. Many knitters find this a very tedious task, but it is well worth putting in the effort. Sew in all ends and don't be tempted to use a long yarn end for sewing up. Always use a separate length of yarn for sewing up. If you make a mistake, you can undo the stitching without the danger of unravelling all your knitting.

Thread a darning needle with the loose end of the yarn, weave the needle along about 5 stitches on the wrong side of the fabric and pull the thread through. Weave the needle in the opposite direction for about 5 stitches, pull the thread through again and cut off the end of the yarn neatly with scissors.

## Making up

There are several ways of joining pieces of knitting, but the most usual are flat seaming with mattress stitch, and back stitch, which makes a raised seam. Flat seaming is used for ribs, but otherwise the two are interchangeable.

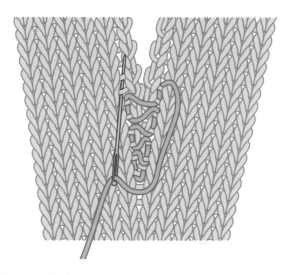

### Mattress stitch

Mattress stitch is a method of joining knitted pieces from the right side of the fabric and is ideal for matching stripes accurately. For the best finish, this stitch should be worked one stitch in from the edge of the knitting (see above).

1 With the right sides of the knitting upwards, lay the pieces to be joined edge to edge. Insert a blunt-tipped needle from the wrong side between the edge stitch and the second stitch. Take the yarn to the opposite piece, insert the needle from the front between the edge stitch and the second stitch, pass the needle under the loops of 2 rows and bring it back through to the front.

**2** Insert the needle under the loops of the corresponding 2 rows in the opposite piece in the same way, and continue this zigzag lacing all along the seam, taking care not to miss any rows and matching any pattern.

**3** Pull the yarn to close the seam, either after each action or after a few stitches. Take care not to pull it too tight, or the seam will pucker, or leave it too loose.

### Back stitch

Back stitch is the other main method of making up a piece of knitting. It is worked from the wrong side of the knitted fabric.

**1** Pin the pieces to be joined with right sides together. Insert a blunt-tipped needle into the knitting at the end, one stitch or row from the edge, then take the needle around the two edges to secure them and bring it back up through the fabric. Insert the needle into the fabric just behind the point at which the previous stitch came out and make a small stitch.

**2** Re-insert the needle where the previous stitch started and bring it up to make a longer stitch. Re-insert the needle where the previous stitch ended. Repeat to the end, taking care to match any pattern.

### Choosing yarns

It is now possible to purchase yarns in two different ways: from yarn shops and via the Internet (search for 'knitting yarns'). Both sources offer a huge range of yarns and other products, such as needles, buttons, beads and other accessories.

If you are a knitting novice, it is a good idea to visit a yarn shop, where you will be amazed at the vast array of yarns available. You will be able to touch the different balls of yarn and examine their textures, become familiar with all the different types available and discuss your requirements with the knowledgeable staff. A good Internet site is a fantastic resource, too: it will display the whole spectrum of colors in a yarn range or ranges and provide plenty of useful knitting information. You will also be able to order shade cards, which will help you get a feel for the yarns available.

The problem comes in deciding which yarns to choose from the multitude available. In the knitting patterns in this book, I have specified the yarn I have used, as it is often the particular texture and/or colors that inspired the design. I have used a variety of different yarn types: some for practical reasons, some because of the color range, and some because they are just so luxurious.

### Substituting yarns

You may wish to substitute the yarn I have used in this book with one of your own choice. You will need to take care if you do this, because all the patterns are worked out mathematically to the specified yarn. If you substitute a yarn, you must achieve the tension/gauge stated in the pattern, or your project will turn out too big or too small.

Yarns come in various weights, such as 4-ply, double knitting and Aran. If you are substituting one yarn for another, look for a similar yarn with the same tension/gauge – this will be stated on the ball band. Always knit a tension/gauge square of your chosen yarn before embarking on the design.

Some yarns are not easy to substitute. For example, I would not recommend the substitution of another yarn for the Rowan Denim used for the Denim-Style Jacket (see page 48) as this yarn is designed to shrink and fade like denim fabric on washing and the pattern is written with this in mind. Likewise, the Fabulous and Felted coat (see page 34) is felted after knitting and other yarns may not felt to the same dimensions as the yarn suggested in this pattern.

Having said all this, it can be fun to substitute yarns and to start thinking creatively about knitting.

# Knitting from a chart

Some of the designs in this book include both written instructions and a chart. To write out the whole pattern would be very complicated, and it is usually just as easy to visualize your knitting as a chart and begin to treat it as a picture, 'painting' with colored yarns.

Reading a chart is easier if you imagine it as the right side of a piece of knitting, working from the lower edge to the top. Each square on the chart represents one stitch, and each line of squares represents one row of knitting. When working from the chart, read odd-numbered rows – 1, 3, 5 etc. (the right side of the fabric) – from right to left, and even-numbered rows – 2, 4, 6 etc. (the wrong side of the fabric) – from left to right.

Each yarn color used is given a letter in the pattern, which corresponds with a symbol on the chart. This is shown in the key that accompanies the chart.

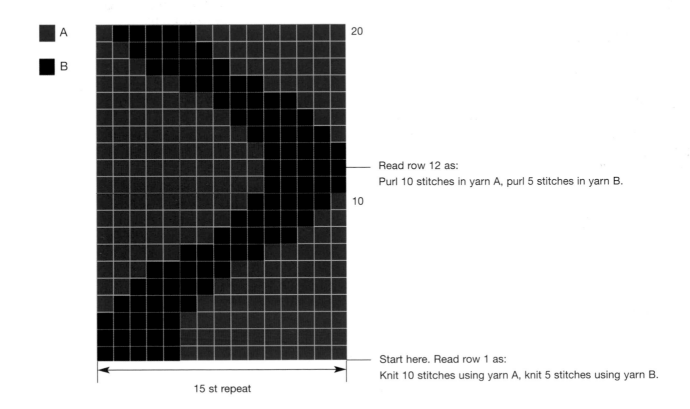

A

B

20

Read row 12 as:
Purl 10 stitches in yarn A, purl 5 stitches in yarn B.

10

Start here. Read row 1 as:
Knit 10 stitches using yarn A, knit 5 stitches using yarn B.

15 st repeat

# Index

# Acknowledgments

## Publisher's Acknowledgments

We would like to thank Barry Blinks at Addiscombe Dog Training for his help with finding such great models, as well as Jason and Sam Bassett, Maureen Blanks, Cath Gray, Mandy Little, Gareth Sambidge, Kim Sullivan and John White for bringing their dogs along.

**Executive Editor**  Katy Denny
**Editor**  Leanne Bryan
**Pattern Checker**  Pauline Hornsby
**Executive Art Editor**  Joanna MacGregor
**Designer**  Grade Design Consultants
**Photographer**  Gareth Sambidge
**Illustrator**  Kuo Kang Chen
**Production Controller**  Nigel Reed
**Picture Library Manager**  Jennifer Veall

## Author's Acknowledgments

I would like to thank the team of knitters – Diane, Joy, Nicky, Anne, Avril and Katy – who didn't laugh (too much) when I asked them to knit dog coats and did a wonderful job. Thanks also go to everyone at Hamlyn for book design, styling, recruiting models – everything that makes a book possible. Finally, the book would be nothing without the efforts and patience of the stunning models and their owners – thank you Parsnip, Chica, Grace, Bly, Poppy, Mica, Bill, Freddie, Lucy and Disco.

Parsnip  Chica  Grace  Bly  Poppy

Mica  Bill  Freddie  Lucy  Disco